PRISON DIARY

PRISON DIARY

Jayaprakash Narayan

Edited with an Introduction by
A. B. Shah

UNIVERSITY OF WASHINGTON PRESS
Seattle and London

Library of Congress Cataloging in Publication Data
Narain, Jai Prakash.
　Prison diary

　Includes index.
　　1. Narain, Jai Prakash. 2. Political prisoners—
India—Biography. 3. India—Politics and government—
1947-　　I. Shah, Amritlal B., 1920-
HV9793.N37　1978　　　　365'.45'0924　　　　78-5471
ISBN 0-295-95613-5

Foreword

Jayaprakash Narayan, popularly known in India as J.P., is an American-educated (Ohio and California universities) political leader who stands head and shoulders above all other politicians in India by virtue of his personal integrity, a rare quality in political life anywhere, and his remarkable dedication to the ideals of human dignity, democracy, and freedom. In India today he has reached near-Gandhian stature.

He came to occupy this unique place in Indian public life after passing through various political stages. He was a Marxist while a student in the United States, a follower of Gandhi on returning to India, later a founder of the Congress Socialist party, and finally a leader of the *Sarvodaya* movement, a constructive, non-political service organization.

A unique thing about Jayaprakash Narayan's life is that he has never sought nor accepted any public office in India. But while he remains outside of party and power politics, he is very much in Indian political life, for his views and utterances on contemporary issues, national and international, transcend narrow loyalties and partisan allegiances and command national attention and respect. He walks somewhat apart from the madding crowd with an enviable detachment, integrity, and sanity. Whenever he has been offered positions by the government, he has declined in the belief that he could serve the nation better if he did not hold public office.

When he took it upon himself to challenge Mrs. Gandhi, then India's Prime Minister, about the tremendous corruption in her federal government, as well as in the Congress party-led state government in his native, backward Bihar State, he could not have realised that his confrontation with the Prime Minister would be total, leading to his prompt imprisonment without trial. From his pre-dawn, secret arrest on June 26, 1975, until his release on

November 12, 1975, a total of 139 days, the frail, ailing leader was held in detention for daring to oppose her and create a mass movement that would challenge Mrs. Gandhi's totalitarian regime.

The present book is a diary he kept in prison. He was subjected to solitary confinement in jail, except for the time when he was a prisoner-patient in government hospitals in New Delhi and Chandigarh. Mrs. Gandhi's dictatorship was so severe that even the doctors who attended him were afraid to say an extra word beyond what their clinical duties demanded. The denial of visitors and all contact with fellow political or other prisoners for long periods during his imprisonment, and the resulting loneliness, were psychologically traumatic. Who can estimate how much this contributed to the breakdown of his health?

But thanks to a few dedicated Indian physicians, and the operations performed by American experts at Seattle, he is still with us. Fortunately, despite having to work against tremendous odds, J.P. lived to see the end of Mrs. Gandhi's dictatorship in the March 1977 parliamentary elections, and the setting up of a new, democratic government with Mr. Morarji Desai, a real and dedicated Gandhian, as India's Prime Minister.

As a human and historical document, Jayaprakash's *Prison Diary* has great value. He writes simply, lucidly, and movingly, recording the agony and pain he felt at what Mrs. Gandhi was doing to the country. The *Diary* opens with the agonising lines, "My world lies in a shambles all around me. I am afraid I shall not see it put together again in my lifetime. May be my nephews and nieces will see that. May be."

Jayaprakash was kept in such strict solitary confinement that British Nobel Peace Prize winners, as well as his near and dear, were not permitted to see him. It is heartbreaking to read in one of his entries: "I have searched my heart and I can say truly that even if I were to die now, I would not mind it. I would surely like to see my dear ones around my death-bed, but long back I have made my peace with death without setting my eyes on them. It is this tightening grip of death on our democracy that makes my heart weep. Is this what we fought for, what we worked for all our life? I think it is this heartache that is retarding my recovery."

When Jayaprakash was in jail, the doctors who examined him gave him no more than three months to live. His illness was considered terminal. There were terrible rumours all over the country of funeral arrangements made by the government of India with state honours to be given posthumously after his cremation at Patna as he was expected to die any day. Jayaprakash, aware of the rumours of these plans, prepared a statement while in hospital about his political position in relation to Mrs. Gandhi's totalitarianism. He was rightly afraid that on his death, Mrs. Gandhi's government would release a statement as from him, falsifying his position and offering his support to her dictatorship. Photostat copies of his secretly prepared personal statement were smuggled out of the country and deposited with such newspapers as *The New York Times*, *The Washington Post* and *The Times* of London. By sheer willpower, Jayaprakash survived and there was no occasion to counter any claim by the government in power that he had changed his mind regarding Mrs. Gandhi's government on the eve of his death.

During the days when he was seriously ill, obituary notices were submitted by some leading Indian newspapers to the government censor. It is tragic to recall that in these obituaries all references to Jayaprakash's role as a freedom fighter, and his lifetime work in the cause of India's political independence and economic advancement, were deleted! History bears witness to the fact that a true and honest record is an embarrassment to dictators.

When Mrs. Gandhi made the miscalculation of her life and ordered general parliamentary elections, releasing the leaders of the opposition, she hardly expected Jayaprakash to live, much less to help unite all the opposition parties. From his sickbed, he helped organize the elections all over the country, winning a thumping majority for the united opposition parties under the name of the Janata party, defeating Mrs. Gandhi and her Congress party. It was nothing short of a physical as well as a political miracle.

Jayaprakash is still with us, and the "total revolution" he preaches may yet come to pass, transforming India into a new polity where political parties do not wrangle for loaves and fishes. It is his dream that all good and able men strive for an honest, nonpartisan government which will give India's long-suffering millions not only political freedom but also emancipation from their age-old economic deprivation. May his dream come true.

S. Chandrasekhar
Vice-Chancellor and President
Annamalai University;
Former Union Minister of Health
and Family Planning, Government
of India

Chidambaram
South India
24 December 1977

Contents

Introduction to the Second Edition

The first edition of this book had to be printed under conditions of censorship at a time when they seemed to have become a long-term feature of life in India. The printing had to be done at night, often in small instalments. Consequently, production standards, including proof-reading, suffered. But there was nothing one could do about it.

This second edition is being produced under conditions of freedom, for which we are grateful to the ordinary, unsophisticated people of India. By their verdict at the polls, they have vindicated the faith that Mahatma Gandhi and the makers of the Indian Constitution placed in them when they introduced universal adult franchise as the basis of the Indian polity.

This edition contains some additional entries, in Hindi, which had to be left out from the first edition. All the entries in Hindi are now given in the Appendix.

We had also hoped to include in this edition an Epilogue by J P. Unfortunately, because of the unremitting pressure on his time and energies, this has not been possible. In its place, we have included the text of his broadcast to the nation on 13 April 1977.

Pune   A. B. Shah
April 15, 1977

Introduction to the First Edition

Mr. Jayaprakash Narayan's *Prison Diary* is a historic document whose significance will outlive the circumstances in which it came to be written. A proper assessment of its contents can only be made after the present Emergency has become part of history. One so close to them and to their chief protagonist as this Editor has been can only react to it in an essentially personal vein. But it is not difficult to see that the *Diary* is more than the musings of a Prometheus in chains. It represents the thinking, the mood and the moral sensitivity of some of the finest minds of contemporary India. In that sense Jayaprakash Narayan's *Prison Diary* is also the diary of millions besides him who a year ago overnight found themselves inmates of the vast prison into which India was converted by Mrs Indira Gandhi's midnight *coup*.

The *Diary* covers a period of less than four months, from July 21 to November 4, 1975 and is presented here with the minimum of editing. The reader will find in it some repetitions, reflections of a strictly personal nature, references to the *Bhagavad Gita* and even a lone excursion in international politics (September 5) which does not fit in with the rest of the *Diary*. But these have all been kept as they were, for they give an insight into the working of the author's mind during the period covered by the *Diary*.

The *Diary* opens with a profoundly moving confession : 'My world lies in a shambles all around me.' But it is not a wail of despair. It is, rather, a frank recognition of the situation after nearly a month of cogitation in solitary confinement. Nor does one find anywhere in it a trace of bitterness or hurt vanity. Instead, one sees an exercise in self-analysis and an analysis of where and why things went wrong. For instance, in the first entry (July 21, 1975) J P asks himself : 'Where have my calculations gone wrong?', and answers : 'I went wrong in assuming that a

Prime Minister in a democracy would use all the normal and abnormal laws to defeat a peaceful democratic movement, but would not destroy democracy itself and substitute for it a totalitarian system. I could not believe that even if the Prime Minister wanted to do it, her senior colleagues and her party, which has had such high democratic traditions would permit it. But the unbelievable has happened.' Later J P was to realise that the 'unbelievable' could happen, and that too without any large-scale resistance, because the democratic tradition had not yet taken root among the common people of India. Steeped in a centuries-old authoritarian culture and weighed down under the burden of poverty and ignorance, they could hardly understand what they had lost. The task of restoring democracy in India would therefore involve not merely a struggle on the political plane but also steady, unostentatious work to educate the people in the values and institutions of democracy at the grass-roots level.

The *Diary* also makes a remarkable attempt at delineating the Gandhian-humanist vision of the good society, and outlines the kind of effort, the 'total revolution', that would be necessary to bring it into existence. This effort need not always assume the form of a confrontation with the government; it may be carried on in cooperation with the government provided the latter is responsive to the people's will and is committed to their welfare. Nor is the struggle to be confined to the political field alone; it will have to be waged on many fronts—social, economic, educational, cultural, even ecological. For, the goal is not merely the weeding out of corruption and providing the necessaries of life to the millions who live below the poverty line. These are only two of the preconditions for restoring man to the dignity to which the Preamble to the Constitution of India entitles him. But much more will have to be done before he is able to live in freedom and self-respect. It is a pity that because of a hectic public life J P could not elaborate his vision, an outline of which he gives in the entry for September 9. Nor, with the damage done to his health during months of solitary confinement, is there much chance of his being able to do so now. One may only hope that some group of intellectuals and social scientists who share his ideas will one day perform this task.

One result of the exercise in self-analysis mentioned above is a convincing justification of what has come to be known as the 'J P movement' and a refutation of the ill-informed, sometimes deliberately mendacious criticism levelled at it. Earlier too, before the proclamation of Emergency, J P had set out his views on more than one occasion in order to allay the misgivings of well-meaning admirers and rebut the charge of instigating violence by the people and a 'rebellion' by the police and the army. But public memory is short, and many who ought to have known better are taken in by this baseless slander. These charges are still being frequently repeated by the government through the press, the radio, television and the documentaries prepared by the Films Division. Indeed, an unremitting campaign of character assassination is being carried on against J P and the institutions with which he has been associated. The *Diary* is therefore indispensable reading for anyone who wishes to know the other side, particularly since nothing that J P or his associates have to say is allowed to be published even when it has no bearing on the stated objects of the Censorship Order.

But the *Diary* is more than a reasoned defence of the J P movement. It is also a record of the manner in which a sensitive mind reacted from day to day to the happenings in a world that lay 'in a shambles'—witness, for example, the entry for August 22 when J P read the 'terrible, terrible news from Bangladesh' of the brutal murder of as many as 18 members of Sheikh Mujib's family; or the entry for August 27 on learning about the unprecedented floods in Patna and some other parts of Bihar. The anguish of these two entries is in sharp contrast to the sense of disgust (September 12) at the hypocritical way Congressmen appear to 'have gone all out to lionise Vinoba' on the occasion of his eightieth birthday, or to the sarcasm of the comment (September 20) on the so-called All-India Conference of Educators for Secularism, Socialism and Democracy.

The most interesting parts of the *Diary* are, of course, those in which J P tries to reconstruct the planning that must have preceded the proclamation of Emergency. He is of the view (July 22, 26) that there must be two plans, to one of which Mrs Gandhi would be privy and which indeed, would have been so cleverly put forward by the Russians through their agents in the Prime Minister's entourage that she would regard it as her own plan; the other plan, which would be put into operation at the appropriate time at a later date, would push her aside once her utility to the Russians is over and convert India into a satellite of the USSR.

That the decision to proclaim a state of Emergency under Art. 352 of the Constitution of India was taken by Mrs Gandhi without the knowledge of the Congress Working Committee, the Cabinet or even the Ministry of Home Affairs is reasonably certain. As far as this writer has been able to ascertain, the Prime Minister had obtained prior clearance from her senior colleagues in the party and the Government, but that was for proclaiming, at a time to be decided by her, a financial emergency under Art. 360 of the Constitution, not a general emergency under Art. 352 as in fact she did. In other words, Mrs Gandhi exceeded her mandate and presented her colleagues with a *fait accompli*. Having proclaimed a general emergency and concentrated all power in her own hands, she no longer needed their support or goodwill. It was they, on the contrary, who were now in mortal fear of her. For, not many of them could boast a clean record or had the courage to stand up to Mrs Gandhi at the risk of being thrown out of office, and even worse. The few who had this quality had already been disposed of on the pretext of party discipline, and time and privilege had corrupted the rest beyond all hope. The iron had entered too deep into their souls.

But J P is not pessimistic about the future. He is aware that 'the betrayal of the intellectuals has started' and 'the rats have begun to leave the sinking ship' (September 21). But 'no matter how far the betrayal of the intelligentsia may go', he has 'unshakable faith in the people and the country's youth and students' (October 1).

The nature of Mrs Gandhi's dictatorship tends to support this view. She has borrowed some of the techniques of communism but seems unwilling to adopt its ideology. One would think she is wise in steering clear of any rigid ideology, for the kind of party that a totalitarian ideology like communism or fascism needs cannot be built up at short notice in India. She has therefore opted for a regime which approximates that of Aurangzeb rather than Stalin or Brezhnev. But as the experience of the post-war period suggests, a non-ideological dictatorship cannot endure in the modern world. Sukarno, Ayub and Nkrumah tried the experiment and their fate should serve as a warning to Mrs Gandhi and others who may aspire to step into her shoes. A dynasty would have a still poorer chance.

What is more likely to happen is that unless the present atmosphere of fear and oppression is lifted and the working of democratic institutions restored, a terrorist movement will gradually develop and plunge India into chaos and violence. It is this prospect which horrifies J P and to which he draws the Prime Minister's attention in his letter of July 21 (Appendix 1). In an appeal that would touch the heart of anyone who loved India, J P says :

You know I am an old man. My life's work is done. And after Prabha's going I have nothing and no one to live for. . . . I have given all my life, after finishing education, to the country and asked for nothing in return. So I shall be content to die a prisoner under your regime.

Would you listen to the advice of such a man ? Please do not destroy the foundations that the Fathers of the Nation, including your noble father, had laid down. There is nothing but strife and suffering along the path you have taken. You inherited a great tradition, noble values and a working democracy. Do not leave behind a miserable wreck of all that. It would take a long time to put all that together again.

J P's appeal is still to evoke a response from the Prime Minister of India.

Pune
June 26, 1976   A. B. SHAH

First

Dear Prime Minister,

I am appalled at press reports of your speeches and interviews. (The very fact that you have to say something every day to justify your action implies a guilty conscience.) Having muzzled the press and every kind of public dissent, you continue with your distortion & untruths without fear of criticism or contradiction. If you think that in this way you will be able to justify yourself in the public eye and doom the Opposition to political perdition, you are sorely mistaken. If you doubt this, you may test it by revoking the emergency, restoring to the people their fundamental rights, restoring the freedom of the press, releasing all those whom you

"सम्पूर्ण क्रांति अब नारा है
जानी इतिहास हमारा है ।।"

क्या अब यह इतिहास का एक भाग
मात्र बन कर रह जायेगा ? सब "जी हुजूर",
कायर, बुजदिल तो जरूर हँसते होंगे हम
पर। "आस्मान के सितारे तोड़ने चले थे,
गिरे हैं अब आंखें नम में"। लेकिन दुनिया
में जो कुछ किया है वह सितारे तोड़नेवालों
ने ही किया है, चाहे भले ही उसके लिये
उन्हें उनको प्राणों का मूल्य चुकाना
पड़ा है।

सम्पूर्ण क्रांति के बदले आज
तो सम्पूर्ण प्रतिक्रांति की चरमोत्कर्ष बेला
है। इस समय तो उल्लू अंगर जीवड़ बड़े
प्रसन्न हैं। चारों तरफ हुआ हुआ और
हूई की आवाज सुनाई देती है। लेकिन काल
चक्र तो घूमता ही रहता है। लेकिन रात
चाहे कितनी ही अंधेरी हो, प्रभात तो-

PRISON DIARY

My world lies in a shambles all round me. I am afraid I shall not see it put together again in my life-time. Maybe my nephews and nieces will see that. May be.

Here was I trying to widen the horizons of our democracy. Trying to do it mainly by involving the people more intimately and continuously in the processes of democracy. This in two ways. One, by creating some kind of machinery through which there could be a measure of consultation with the people in the setting up of candidates. Two, by providing a machinery—the same machinery as in One above would have done—through which the people could keep a watch on their representatives and demand good and honest performance from them. These were the two drops of essence that I wanted to distil out of all the clang and clamour of the Bihar movement. And here am I ending up with the death of democracy.

Where have my calculations gone wrong ? (I almost said "our" calculations, but that would be wrong. I must bear the full, the whole, responsibility.) I went wrong in assuming that a Prime Minister in a democracy would use all the normal and abnormal laws to defeat a peaceful democratic movement, but would not *destroy* democracy itself and substitute for it a totalitarian system. I could not believe that even if the Prime Minister wanted to do it, her senior colleagues and her party, which has had such high democratic traditions, would permit it. But the unbelievable has happened. One could have understood such a result if there had been a violent outbreak and there was fear of a violent take-over. But a peaceful movement resulting in such a denouement ! What can the people do, the youth do to fight against corruption, unemployment, poverty ? Wait quietly for the next general elections ! But what if in the meantime the situation becomes intolerable ? Then what are the people to do ? Sit quietly and fold up their arms and silently bear their miseries ? That would be Mrs Gandhi's image of democracy : silence of the grave. And what if the elections themselves are neither free nor fair ? For that they must awaken and organise. I do not think in any democratic society the people have relied wholly and solely on elections to change their plight. Everywhere there have been strikes, protests, marches, sit-ins, sit-outs, etc.

There is no need here to recount the steps taken by the Prime Minister to strangle democracy to death and clamp down her dictatorial regime. Here was this same Prime Minister who used to accuse us time and again of wanting to destroy democracy and establish fascism. And here we see the same Prime Minister destroying democracy and establishing fascism herself in the name of the same democracy. She is saving democracy by murdering it with her own hands and burying the corpse deep down in the grave. Has she not declared that India cannot afford to go back to the pre-emergency state of licence ? Licence ! She has the cheek to talk of licence. Has she forgotten the Congress youth rally convened by her in Delhi (on 9th August 1974) ? What vandalism and vulgarity were abroad ! And does she remember the all-India people's march and rally of 6th March 1975 ?[1] The Inspector-General of Police, Delhi, himself had said that there was no incident on that day. And what about the shameful affair in Calcutta (on 2nd April 1975) in front of the University Institute hall where I was to address a meeting ? And, in complete contrast, does she remember that massive Calcutta march of June 5 of the same year ? It was universally acclaimed as the most peaceful event of its kind in that sorely disturbed city. I do not know if public meetings, processions, bandhs—all peaceful and orderly—were or can ever be evidence of licence.

I wonder what all those ladies and gentlemen are saying now who used to tell me that I was the only "hope" for the country. Are they invoking curses on my head for bringing about this terrible doom ? I should not be surprised. They may even be saying that hemmed in from all sides as Mrs Gandhi was, she

1. This was an all-India march organised by the people's movement in which, according to different estimates, from one half to one million people had participated.

2   PRISON DIARY

could not but act in the manner she has. But I hope there are some people at least, particularly among the young who may still be loyal to me and to the cause I represented. They are the hope of the future. India will arise from the grave, no matter how long it might take.

I had always believed that Mrs Gandhi had no faith in democracy, that she was by inclination and conviction a dictator. My belief has tragically turned out to be true. I recall that when in an article or statement I had quoted Mrs Gandhi's biographer (Mrs Uma Vasudeva) as proof of my belief, the poor author was made to explain away what she had written. But that did not change my mind.

Where then did I go wrong? Events have shown that my mistake was in assuming that, whatever Mrs Gandhi's personal inclination, it would not be possible for her to become a dictator. First, I thought that the people would not allow it and she would have no courage to go ahead. Second, I thought that the Congress party, as I wrote yesterday, would not let that happen. Well, events have proved me wrong. I still think that popular resistance will grow and gather strength. It will take time. At present the people are dazed and being deprived of their leaders do not know what to do. But new leaders will be thrown up from amongst those whom I mentioned yesterday, i.e. an entirely new leadership will grow up and the opposition will continue.

As for the Congress party, I do not understand its spinelessness. Of course, quite a number of Congressmen are disguised communists. They will go with Mrs Gandhi to the ultimate end. They have always been enemies of democracy. Behind them is the Right CPI and behind it is Soviet Russia. Russia has backed Mrs Gandhi to the hilt. Because the farther Mrs Gandhi advances on her present course, the more powerful an influence will Russia have over this country. A time may come when, having squeezed the juice out of Mrs Gandhi, the Russians through the CPI and their Trojan horses within the Congress will dump her on the garbage heap of history and instal in her place their own man. May be Mrs Gandhi herself has become a stooge, but she loves power and would not like to be forced out of it. But a time may come, *will* come I believe, when her utility would have been exhausted and one dyed deeper in communist colours and a more willing tool would be considered desirable. At that point Mrs Gandhi would find herself helpless. I am not suggesting that all this is inevitably going to happen. May be the people would rise, the army may oppose and take over itself. There may be other possibilities.

But what about the other Congressmen, who may be called true Congressmen? Why have they meekly submitted? It seems that there are in reality very few true Congressmen. And after the arrest of Chandrashekar and Ramdhan and the excommunication of the other Young Turks, these true Congressmen also have not courage enough to rebel. Most of the others have no ideological convictions and are poor self-seekers and *jee-huzurs* (yes-men). They will be used by Mrs Gandhi and then pushed aside. But what about the senior Congress leaders such as Jagjivan Ram, Chavan, Swaran Singh? I cannot believe that like Mrs Gandhi they too are enemies of democracy. Perhaps they too lack courage and do not like to lose their jobs and end up in detention. Or perhaps they are biding their time. I do not know. There is also another factor: they are disunited amongst themselves. But I an mortified by their silent acquiescence.

That India too should become another Pakistan or Bangladesh! What a shame that would be! These countries did not have a Gandhi, a Nehru, a Patel, a Rajendra Prasad, a Maulana Azad, a Rajgopalachari. Will all their work be reduced to ashes? It is difficult to believe it. That is why I said yesterday Indian democracy will rise from its grave.

July 25

Did not feel like writing the last two days. Every nail driven deeper into the coffin of Indian democracy is like a nail driven into my heart. I have searched my heart and I can say truly that even if I were to die now, I would not mind it. I would surely like to see my dear ones around my death-bed, but long back I have made my peace with death without setting my eyes on them. It is this tightening grip of death on our democracy that makes my heart weep. Is this what we fought for, what we worked for all our life? I think it is this heart-ache that is retarding my recovery. The ECG this morning showed again the appearance of ectopic beats, and I have been put again on dialintine.

Raja [2] came yesterday. And after him Vimal Dave, junior to Tarkunde.[3] Raja is petitioning the Supreme Court against my being kept alone and his prayer is that I be allowed 'acceptable' company.

I spoke to Mr Dave about my request to the Union Home Secretary for my transfer either to Bihar or to a place nearer to it than Chandigarh. Lal Babu [4] had come from Calcutta and Raja from Bombay. Both so far away from here. I want to see Babuni [5] and she also wants to see me. But how far is Patna from here and how troublesome the journey!

This is all that I can write today. Maybe, the mood will change tomorrow and I might write some more.

July 26

Today I have completed one full month of my detention. I must say this one month has been like a year. Maybe, it is due to the break in the habit of jail-going for 30 years, more correctly 29 years. Indiraji's regime may be remembered in history for its many achievements or lack of them—its most notable achievement is the murder of democracy—but for me it will be remembered (for the few months or years I remain alive) as a regime in

2. Rajeshwar Prasad, J P's younger brother who lives in Bombay.
3. V. M. Tarkunde, former judge of Bombay High Court, now senior counsel in the Supreme Court of India; a former associate of the late Manabendranath Roy.
4. Lal Babu, pet name of Shivnath Prasad, brother of J P's deceased wife, Prabhavati Devi.
5. Babuni, pet name of J P's younger sister.

independent India in which I experienced for the first time tear gas, lathi blows (of the CRP) and detention. Under British rule I had not personally ever experienced tear gas or lathi blows. And since my release from detention in April 1946 from Agra Central Prison I had never been arrested or detained. Another reason for the month appearing to me as a year is, I am sure, my loneliness. The company of other detenus might have helped.

However, it is not this that I sat down to record today. It is something much more important, though every sensible Indian must have come to the same decision which I have reached and which I record below.

It might appear from my letter to the Prime Minister[6] and my notes of the two subsequent days that she acted in the manner she has done when her position as PM was threatened. That only determined the timing. But I am sure Indiraji, the disguised communists in her party, the CPI and, behind the scene, Soviet agents must have prepared a detailed plan for substituting a totalitarian system for the democratic one that we had until 25th June. To all three of them—the PM, the communist stooges in the Congress and the CPI—democracy was anathema and they were planning for long years the steps by which their goal could be reached : first "social democracy" and then naked communist party rule under carefully disguised Russian tutelage.

There must be two plans instead of one. One, to which Indiraji is privy and is made to believe that it is her plan. In this plan Indiraji is always at the top till death intervenes. The other plan is a Soviet plan which the CPI has been made to believe has emerged from their own brilliant heads. This plan is not known to Indiraji though she might have some private suspicions. It is also not known to the communist stooges in the Congress, except a very few whom the Soviets trust and who by their outward actions have never shown any sympathy for the CPI or even the Soviets. They might even have appeared at times to be critical, if not hostile, to the fatherland of socialism.

The latter plan was to take effect at the point of transition from social democracy to undisguised communist dictatorship. Many heads were then to roll, though in the social democratic period

6. Written on 21 July; See Appendix 1.

too head-rolling would not be such an outlandish matter.

The point is, will this plan, or *these* plans succeed? I doubt very much. But better not speculate about it now. In any case, this country will go through hell for some time.

The question is, could we have avoided this catastrophe? I have dealt with this question before, but it bobs up again and again like King Charles' head. Well, we could have staved it off, if we had behaved as good boys, contended ourselves with passing resolutions and waiting upon the high and mighty with petitions. Is that the meaning of *Anushasan Parva*? I wonder! I recall Vinobaji had advised me, while waging a struggle against social and economic injutice and evil, to desist from a struggle against the government. But his reason was that with America arming Pakistan again and China also helping (more with words than with military hardware), there was a possibility of a conflict with Pakistan and so a struggle against the government would weaken the country and therefore a struggle against the government was not advisable. I put forward my own arguments, which will be found in the account of our conversation circulated by the Sarva Seva Sangh among a few selected persons. However, Vinobaji was not persuaded, nor was I.[7]

But what do we have now? Not a war with Pakistan but a deliberate, pre-planned and ghastly murder of Indian democracy. Vinobaji had not given even a hint of this. I wonder if he considers that a totalitarian dictatorship is a healthy course of discipline, a sort of fire of purification, through which the country and particularly hotheads like me, Morarji Desai, Siddharaj,[8] and a host of others must pass so that India may become strong enough to face her enemies and also to make progress towards moral, material and spiritual fulfilment.

So if everyone behaved decently, the Opposition, the wrong-headed Sarvodaya workers, the students and other youth and the people themselves, that is to say, if there had been something

7.   The reference is to the discussion which took place between J P and Acharya Bhave in the morning of 14th March 1975 at Paunar, Wardha, where the latter lives. It was during this discussion that Acharya broke for a few minutes his vow of year-long silence.

8.   Siddharaj Dhadda, President of the Sarva Seva Sangh, also in detention.

approaching the silence of the grave in the country, everything would have been well and our democracy would have been safe and sound. But what worth would have that democracy been ? In a democracy what ways are there for bringing about social, economic, cultural and political changes ? Are elections the only means ? And what if elections are neither free nor fair ? And how can elections be won by keeping your mouth shut and your hands folded ? And how do you fight against injustice and oppression ? And what do you do with a corrupt and misruling government ? Wait until the elections and lose ? If you do not expose such a government, if you do not agitate for its removal and replacement, what chances have you to win at the hustings ? All these meetings, demonstrations, strikes, bandhs, civil disobedience, etc., are the weapons of de-mocracy and they have to be used. True, it must be done in a peaceful and orderly manner. Disorder and violence do not go with democracy. But the Bihar movement was eminently peaceful and orderly. And the demonstrations in Delhi. The seven days' civil disobedience programme also was to be peacefully conducted. There was no cause for the proclamation of the Emergency, the suppression of the press, the suspension of fundamental rights, the arrests and detention of thousands and the several amend-ments to the Constitution, the People's Representation Act and MISA. All this I have argued at length in my letter to the P M.

All that has been done by Indiraji since 26th June is just an unfoldment of the plan of which I have spoken at the outset.

July 27

Another happy day for me. Babuni and Ashok [9] came. Babuni looked tired and much in apprehension about me. She was on the point of breaking down and crying, which had started to affect me too, but in order to divert her and myself I began to talk to Ashok about his children and sister (my nieces). That suc-ceeded and Babuni took control of herself.

9. Son of J P's younger sister, Babuni.

I was glad to have news of friends and relations in Patna and of the Mahila Charkha Samiti.

I am not in a mood to record my thoughts and comments today.

August 6

The expected has happened. Mrs Gandhi has insured herself against a possible adverse judgment of the Supreme Court by amendments to the Representation of the People Act. A drastic constitutional amendment is also expected. All this is to complete the dictatorship of the self-appointed saviour of the country. All this is said to be done according to the Constitution. Hitler too used the democratic process to establish his fateful dictatorship. Will India also have to go through hell to emerge again from this darkness ? It seems certain now. But the price India will have paid will be crippling. May God help her.

(*Translated from Hindi*)   **August 7**

"Total Revolution is our slogan; Future history belongs to us."

Will this now remain an irony of history ? All *jee-huzurs*, cowards and sycophants must be laughing at us. "They dared to get at the stars but descended into hell", this is how they may be ridiculing us. But only those who sought to get at the stars have achieved anything in the world, may be at the cost of their lives.

Instead of total revolution, we find today the dark clouds of total counter-revolution encircling us. It is a feast day for the owls and jackals whose hoots and growls we hear on all sides. But, howsoever dark the night may be, the dawn is bound to follow.

But will the dawn follow all by itself ? And shall we simply wait, arms crossed ? If social revolution were just to follow the revolutions of nature, there would have been no place for human effort for social progress and change. What then are we to do ? The answer is : "They who raised that slogan and sang that song must offer to sacrifice themselves. And the first to kiss the altar must be the one who was their leader." Doubts have been set at rest; the decision has been taken.

Last night while offering prayers to goddess Bhagwati I had asked for a way out of this darkness, and I got it this morning. My mind is now calm and composed.

In the evening of life

After Prabha's [10] departure I had lost interest in life. Had I not developed a special aptitude for public work, I would have retired to the Himalayas. My heart wept within, but outwardly I followed the routine of life. My health too was deteriorating. It was in this hour of dejection that something unexpected happened which lit up my inner self. My health also started improving, and I experienced a new energy and zeal.

It was in the last months of 1973, when I was at Paunar, that I felt an inner urge to give a call to youth; I addressed an appeal to them and sent it for publication in newspapers under the title "Youth for Democracy". This appeal evoked a more encouraging response than I had expected.

(Translated from Hindi)   **August 11**

My earlier decision [11] stands. The letter [12] was not sent. I destroyed it. I would wait for the proper time and see how the situation develops.

August 11

Have started to read the newspapers again.[13] Mrs Gandhi con-

10. Mrs Prabhavati Devi, wife of the author.
11. The decision to go on an indefinite fast, which was later postponed.
12. The letter conveying the above decision to the Prime Minister.
13. J P had stopped reading newspapers because they contained only one-sided propaganda full of lies let loose by the Government after having silenced the voice of opposition.

PRISON DIARY

tinues to attack and malign me. She says that I have been an opponent of parliamentary democracy, suggesting that I am a believer in dictatorship. Every time she or her colleagues say this they conveniently forget that (a) I have been advocating certain electoral reforms (such as measures to make elections less expensive) to make our parliamentary democracy more democratic, and (b) that I have been advocating a better type of democracy such as Gandhian communitarian democracy or, if that is too idealistic (which it is not), something like a mix of the (German) 'List system' and the majority system that we have here.

Only a few months before my arrest a committee which I had appointed as president of the Citizens for Democracy had consulted the political parties (the ruling Congress did not cooperate), political scientists and non-party public figures and presented a report on amendments to the present system. This report was considered by the Opposition parties and they produced an agreed set of recommendations to which Mrs Gandhi and her party never responded. All this is known to the people and also to the foreign press, to which Mrs Gandhi has been giving so many interviews. But under the emergency, even if someone wanted to reply to her lies, no paper would dare publish it.

In an interview to a foreign newspaper (German, I believe) or maybe in a statement only two or three days ago, Mrs Gandhi castigated the foreign press for attacking her totalitarian moves but not speaking anything about China, etc. Can anything be more juvenile ? The answer is obvious.

I had wanted to comment on what Mrs Gandhi has been saying almost everyday. But having given serious thought to it, I have come to the conclusion that that would be a waste of time. I would better write my own thoughts as and when the spirit moves me. I am convinced that neither the people of India nor of the Western democracies will ever be persuaded to swallow her fibs. She herself has experienced this in the past and has vented her impotent rage over it. An example of this was when at the L. N. Mishra condolence meeting at the Vithalbhai Patel hall she shrieked out, 'even if I were to be killed they would say that I myself had got it done'.

Mrs Gandhi's appeal and Raj Narain's cross-appeal were taken up on the 11th. The case was postponed to 25th. Shanti Bhushan argued that the recent amendments to the law and the Constitution affected the 'basic structure' of the Constitution, which the Court had earlier held was not within Parliament's power. Mr Shanti Bhushan is undoubtedly a great lawyer. Mr Niren De[14] conceded that if it was shown that the Constitution's basic structure had been affected, the matter could be gone into. This is a remarkable development. There still seems to be hope. Some vitality still remains in our democracy. De has asked the Court to define 'basic structure'. That is good. To a layman with commonsense and some understanding of our Constitution and of parliamentary democracy, there is no doubt that the recent amendments, the Emergency proclamation, etc., have not only affected the basic structure of the Constitution, but destroyed it.

When I wrote earlier about the amendments, a very important point had escaped me. This was brought to my attention today. According to our Constitution, there is no direct election of the Prime Minister. Only members of the Lok Sabha are elected. And no one knows beforehand which party or parties will win and who will be subsequently elected as leader of the winning party or parties. This means all MPs are elected alike and the law applies to them equally. Now, when one of them becomes PM, how can his or her election be not challenged as that of any other MP? He or she has not been elected directly as PM—there is no such provision in the Constitution. Therefore this particular amendment is stupid. Mr Gokhale[15] and other members of the Cabinet seem to be mesmerised by the PM as a rabbit by the python. Apart from being stupid, which under the law is not illegal, to exclude the PM's election which takes place after the general election from the jurisdiction of the election law is a piece of discrimination as between one

14. Advocate-General of the Government of India.
15. H. R. Gokhale, Law Minister in the Government of India.

MP and another, which is highly illegal and improper. There is no election of the Prime Minister as such but only of MPs, one of whom might become PM. Therefore, excluding the particular MP's election who later becomes PM from the jurisdiction of the electoral law and the Courts will be discrimination between MPs and MPs.

August 14

Professor Ishwari Prasad in his *History of Muslim Rule* writes about Aurangzeb's death : 'Deprived of that tender nursing and devoted care which reduces half the misery of a patient, when he is surrounded by his own kith and kin, the emperor felt lonely and bitter, but he must pay the penalty of his exalted office.' (p. 653). (Kambakhsh, Aurangzeb's beloved son.)

The Delhi High Court has rejected my petition and for the same reasons as apprehended. I have no complaint against the learned judges. Perhaps none of them has ever been in prison or detention, though some of them might have been in hospital. Ordinarily when one is in hospital, apart from the doctors and nurses, one also has some near or dear one or a friend by one's side. That is half the treatment. Here, in one of the best hospitals in India, the doctors and nurses, who are uniformly kind, come and go as the treatment requires. In freedom, even doctors and nurses could be company. But here they dare not stay a minute longer than necessary. And they would not talk of anything else but the condition of my health. And except for the Director, as soon as any other doctor or one of the nurses enters my room, there follows closely the jail or police (maybe also the IB [16] or CBI [17])—they are all parked here on the entire floor occupying several rooms—representative (a head sepoy perhaps) who keeps standing at my door all the 24 hours (they take turns). It is the same with the administrative officers who occasionally come to see me. They too are tight-lipped

16. Intelligence Branch of the Government of India.
17. Central Bureau of Investigation.

and will talk only about what duty dictates. Thus, while I am in hospital and am being well looked after and while a number of persons cóme and go, I am really alone. And company is what I need most. Everyday there is something in the papers that completely upsets me—usually it is Mrs Gandhi's half-truths and lies. If there had been even one political detenu with me—he could be easily kept in one of the rooms of this part of the floor—we could talk together and vent our feelings. That would have been worth many tablets and sedatives and tranquillizers. Until a few days ago, more precisely till the day I wrote in these pages that I had decided not to bother to comment upon what Mrs Gandhi chose to say, I used to get so upset that sometimes I had to ring for a dose of tranquillizer. But I have got over that stage now. Yet the need of a companion with whom one could talk freely is really great. There can be no question, of course, of one of my kith and kin living with me. So this for me is truly solitary confinement. Day and night —except for the times I am taken out for short walks in the enclosed, stuffy corridor of this floor—I have to keep within my room.

I have spent years in jails during British rule. Unless one was given a solitary cell as punishment one had freedom all day, until lock-up time, to meet with other fellow-prisoners in one's yard, play games, discuss, read together and do whatever one pleased within the rules of the jail. Even when one fell ill and was sent to the jail hospital there were other fellow-prisoners from other yards too and that was a delight. Only in the Lahore Fort I was kept in solitary confinement for a few months. In between there was a *habeas corpus* petition, letters to Government, etc. And finally one day, to the great delight and surprise of both of us, they brought Rammanohar [18]—who had been brought to the Fort a few months after me—to my cell. After that we met everyday for an hour until our transfer together to the Agra Central jail where we were kept together in a big hall or barrack.

Therefore, the assumption of the learned judges that being in hospital there was no penal solitary confinement for me is wrong.

18. The late Dr. Rammanohar Lohia.

But it requires a great deal of human sympathy and imagination to appreciate this. I am not suggesting that the learned judges are lacking in either of these virtues, but the presumptions on which they rejected my petition were wrong.

At the top of this note there is a quotation from Ishwari Prasad's *History of Muslim Rule*. What the Emperor felt, a humble person like me could be allowed to feel.

By the way, Aurangzeb did not pay the price of his exalted office but of his own misdeeds earlier in imprisoning his father and having his brothers and nephews killed. As Professor Ishwari Prasad has himself said, Aurangzeb did not trust his sons and daughters to be near him and with tears in his eyes he himself had sent away his beloved son Kambakhsh for the safety of the latter. Aurangzeb's loneliness was self-chosen, mine is imposed upon me. It is more galling. I am not dying, it is true, though there is no telling about a heart patient. Nevertheless, to be shut up like this when the country is being pushed ever deeper down the abyss of personal dicatorship, is no less than death for me.

(Translated from Hindi)   **August 15**

It is the 15th of August today. Twenty-eight years of our freedom are complete. India is independent of foreign domination, although the direction in which Mrs Gandhi is moving is bound to land this country into the Russian sphere of influence. An article by K. P. S. Menon in today's *Tribune* is a pointer to that horrible future. But I am confident that the people of India will never accept it.

The struggle for freedom was not fought simply for national independence. The establishment of democracy in free India was also an important goal of the struggle. It was in view of this goal that the Constituent Assembly had drawn up a constitution for democratic India and adopted it on 26th November 1949 on behalf of the Indian people. India was accordingly declared a republic on 26th January 1950.

Is anything left of that democracy today ? All this appears to be so unreal and dreamlike that the President and the Prime Minister have to reassure the people again and again that the Emergency is a temporary affair, that India can remain united only under a democracy, etc., etc. The two dignitaries have repeated these assurances in their Independence Day messages today.

But the lame and false arguments, on whose basis the Emergency was proclaimed, and the constitutional amendments that followed lead to the conclusion that these arguments are just an eyewash. So far as Mrs Gandhi is concerned, she does not believe in democracy and she will try her best to prevent its being restored. It has to be seen how far the democratic forces in the country would allow this conspiracy to succeed. If I have rightly understood the people of India and her youth, I have no doubt that they will never let this happen.

There is one more reason to justify this hope. We find that the Prime Minister has been repeating again and again that in view of India's diversities, her large area and huge population, our national unity can endure only in a democratic atmosphere. She has said it again even today. We are now under Mrs Gandhi's dictatorship. But history is witness to the fact that the effort to govern the whole of India from a single centre was never fully successful. Nor could such (centralised) states last for long. There always were kings and sultans, more or less powerful and near-sovereign in their respective regions, under a great emperor. The borders of the various (Indian) empires shrank or expanded as time passed, and within a few centuries the empires disintegrated.

This was the state of affairs even when there was no concept of democracy based on adult franchise, or of civil liberties and rights of every common citizen. Nor was the population of India so large in those days. I do not find any such personal quality in Indiraji or in her party as to believe that her autocratic rule over this vast land will continue for long.

I have spoken above of Mrs Gandhi's party. This party is full of self-seekers and cowards. Corruption is ingrained in a majority of them. There are among them endless quarrels based on selfish motives. Casteism is also there. Can the dictatorial rule of such

16

a party be stable ? All the sincere and courageous ones in the Congress have been thrown out by Indiraji.

If the opposition parties had been united, the Congress rule would have ended long ago. I hope the Opposition, having passed through the fire of dictatorship, will unite now. In fact, one of the reasons that contributed to the proclamation of Emergency was that after the victory of the Janata Front in Gujarat Mrs Gandhi felt that there was a possibility of opposition unity at the national level, in which case she might not win the next election to the Lok Sabha. Moreover, the impact of the Bihar movement was spreading to other states. The success of my countrywide tours might also have frightened her. In such situation, she might have decided that her interest lay in destroying democracy itself. However, as would be clear from what I have said above, she will never succeed in this satanic attempt.

(Translated from Hindi)   **August 16**

Professor Satyavrat in his commentary on the *Bhagavadgita* says (p. 201) 'At the time the Gita was composed, there was a controversy over *Karmakand* versus *Jnanakand*.' In this context, he has mentioned the name of Shankaracharya. This does not seem proper. He should have given the names of some at least of the supporters of each side.

August 16

Terrible news from Bangladesh. It seems incredible. But this is the result of the personal and party dictatorship Mujib had established, banning all other parties. Rumours were thick in Delhi at that time that the whole strategy followed by Mujib had been worked out at Delhi with Mujib's trusted men. At that time Mujib also gave out excuses similar to those being given now by Mrs Gandhi. It was also rumoured at the time of the Mujib *coup* that India too was to go the Bangladesh way, that is, if Mrs Gandhi had her way. India is half way today between democracy and the Mujib dictatorship. I had strong suspicions that Mrs Gandhi would march onward along that path. I have said "had" (in the previous sentence) because of the 'army *coup*'. (God knows if it was an army *coup*, but Khondkar Mushtaq Ahmed could not have brought it about by himself. The CPI is going to say that the Americans have done this ghastly thing. The Russians will most probably keep quiet themselves, but they will certainly encourage their stooges around the world, particularly in Asia, to put the whole thing to American imperialism.) I do fervently hope, may God guide her at this critical moment, that she will realise that dictatorship will ruin this country; that democracy, which she herself said yesterday was necessary to keep India united, must be restored, that the danger to this country that has emerged out of the Bangladesh calamity can be met only if freedom is restored to the people and they are allowed to breathe freely. Suppression of freedom, attempts to prolong the present suffocating situation will only result in frightful consequences. The consequences may be of several kinds; it is not difficult to imagine them. What is needed is not to let them happen. Will Mrs Gandhi rise to the occasion ? Hitherto she has seemed capable to act only when her personal position has been in peril. Can she act when the country itself is in peril ?

August 17

I think I did not do justice yesterday to the tragic happenings in Bangladesh. Mr Mushtaq Ahmed, of course, talks of corruption and suppression of freedom under the previous government and is promising to improve both. That history will show. If he is merely a tool of the army, I do not see how he can do it.

I recall the time when Mujib, having been released by Bhutto, returned to his country to lead it and became Bangabandhu— even Bangapita. He was truly beloved of his people.... At that time I remember writing to him literally with tears in my eyes. I must have written to him two or three letters, to which he replied once or twice. He also sent me very kind words through

Sen.[19] That was how I felt about Mujib in those days. But after his *coup* and establishment of one-party rule, my ardour for him vanished. I realised his difficulties. But if he had the ability, then with his great influence with the people and his supreme authority, like that of Jawaharlal's, he could have brought the situation under control without suppression of democracy. But he acted foolishly and failed. I was sad yesterday when I read of his being killed, but there was no shock, nor in my heart did I grieve much for him.

I never met Mujib in person. Except for him I knew rather intimately all the other political and military leaders of Bangladesh at the time of the Provisional Government. I knew Khondkar Mushtaq Ahmed then. My recollection of him is of a slim person of average height who always sported, non-Bengali like, a cap. It was apparent then that he was not on good terms with Tajuddin Ahmed and also perhaps with Nazrul Islam. Sen reported to me after his return from Bangladesh that Mushtaq Ahmed was alienated—in exile in India he had appeared to be as ardent an admirer of Mujib as the other leaders—from Mujib, perhaps because he was not given the foreign office or another equally important cabinet job. Sen also told me that in the Awami League and in the country generally, if there was anyone who could challenge Mujib's leadership it was Khondkar Mushtaq Ahmed. Who knew that this was the way in which the challenge was to come and succeed ? ... One last word : I had formed two impressions of Ahmed, that he was somewhat pro-Western and a little more Muslim—in the sectarian sense—than the others.

There is a lot of mystery about the Bangladesh *coup* and doubts and questions. Maybe time will answer some of them. But not all, I am afraid.

August 18

I am relieved to read in the papers today that Bangladesh still retains its official name of 'People's Republic' and has not been

19. A. C. Sen, a close associate of JP.

changed to 'Islamic Republic'. Secularism seems to be safe for the time being. In Ahmed's cabinet there are two Hindu ministers —the same as were in Mujib's. I am glad nationalism also remains. Bangladesh is not going to become anyone's satellite. Nor does there seem to be a possibility of any constitutional links forged with Pakistan—confederation, association or anything else like that. As far as I have understood Ahmed he should want India's friendship, but no kind of dependence or inequality in relationship.

Whether democracy and socialism, two of the four creeds or principles on which Mujib based his country's State, will also survive even in name is doubtful. Democracy had been destroyed by Mujib himself, so it is now a question not of its survival but of its revival. Socialism, of course, in Bangladesh as in Congress India, is a slogan and nothing else.

As I predicted yesterday Russia and the Russian press are silent or non-committal. But the communist press in Europe has reacted as predicted by me. *L'humanite* is the most explicit : it is the CIA that has done it. Papers of the Eastern European countries are divided : some look at it as a rightist *coup* with the secret help of the US, and others as an act of extremists backed by China. Yugoslavia only regrets the eclipse of the policy of non-alignment for which Mujib stood. Western papers are not reported much in the *Tribune* which I am given here. But they seem to be much in the dark or undecided. The Islamic Republic canard was the doing of an American press agency. Why should Americans be always up to this kind of mischief ? I have not seen comments of the Indian press yet. As everything else, these comments will also be censored. This means that all comments pointing the finger at the CIA will be published, but perhaps not any balanced view. The CIA and the KGB are both powerful and active everywhere in the world. In India the KGB seems to be doing better; it is quite possible the CIA got the better of the KGB in Bangladesh. My own hunch is that the Bangladesh affair was a domestic event, but why the armed services should have rebelled against Mujib in this brutal fashion is difficult to understand. It is also difficult to understand how the whole thing worked so smoothly. There does not seem to have been much blood spilled in the country or any dissensions in the armed forces.

August 18

I propose to note down in these pages one thought, everyday or on any day I feel like doing it, about the people's movement. Taken together they will constitute my total view of the movement. The notes may have to be re-arranged and edited.

I remember Vinobaji saying to me, when he briefly broke his silence,[20] that he agreed with my concept of struggle and was prepared to help me there, but that I should give up the idea of a struggle against the government. His objection to the latter struggle was that there was danger of war—in view of Pakistan's attitude, American supply of arms once again to Pakistan (the embargo having been lifted) and China's going out of the way to show its friendship for Pakistan. The struggle against the government might weaken the country. Vinobaji did not apprehend that the struggle might end in the strangulation of Indian democracy.

This may be a good starting point for these notes.

The struggle, the movement, was for total revolution, i.e., revolution in every sphere of social life and organisation. The revolution being peaceful, it was not to happen suddenly and swiftly. It would take time, but the times being revolutionary, not too much time—perhaps a space of a decade or two. The basic systemic changes would happen first and the individual and group adaptations, mostly psychological, later.

This should make it clear that a revolutionary change of the political system was an integral and inescapable part of the total revolution and therefore of the struggle.

Perhaps Vinobaji held and still holds that systemic change in the political order could be brought about without a struggle, even a peaceful struggle. But my experience of years of *gram swarajya* (village self-government) work has convinced me that

20. On 14 March 1975; See entry for 26 July, fn 7.

gram swarajya is a valuable political organisation in itself provided it works and is not only on paper. But the gram swarajya movement was not capable of bringing about a systemic political revolution. Theoretically, there is no reason why it should not. I do not know at how many hundreds, maybe thousands, of meetings I had shown how, based on gram swarajya, the new polity would rise and displace the present one. I am not aware that any of my Sarvodaya colleagues, including those who are my severe critics now, ever found fault with my presentation. Districts were taken up, then CD (Community Development) blocks (as in the Saharsa district of Bihar) to build the model, but nowhere has success been achieved.

If we look at the task of total revolution from the narrow and doctrinaire (though never admitted as such) Sarvodaya point of view, it will be seen that the *gram jana-sangharsha samitis* ('Village Committees for People's Struggle') in Bihar were performing the same function as of gram swarajya and many of them were active and were not only on paper. As the struggle deepened, more and more of the samitis would have become active and developed into real *janata sarkars* ('People's Government' at the village level). The gram swarajya movement, beginning with Bhoodan (land-gift) and passing through Gramdan (these were intended to be a sort of groundwork for the gram swarajya to come), has taken more than 20 years to reach the ineffectual state in which it is found today.

On the other hand, the *gram jana-sangharsha samitis* had hardly a few months in which to come to life and yet in many places they were much more real than gram swarajya. The reason I believe is the atmosphere of struggle. It seems to me that in such an atmosphere psychological forces are created that attract men and drive them to accept challenges and to change themselves and change others. In the placid atmosphere in which gram swarajya was working, such psychological forces remained dormant. Spiritual and moral appeals, the saintly influence of Vinobaji, did bring about some remarkable moral changes in some individuals. But they never became a social or psychological force. During the Bhoodan movement when hundreds of thousands of landlords donated their land, it might be claimed that a really widespread moral force, not confined to only a few, was created. Perhaps it was so. But it was short-lived and later uncounted donors took back, or tried to take back, what they had given. That moral force was soon dissipated—though Vinobaji was still in the field—and when gramdan came along there was little of that force remaining. Some of the ideas about land and property remained, but not as accepted ideas. Had the latter been the case, those ideas could have become a tremendous force for social change.

It should not be deduced from the above that the atmosphere of struggle can be conjured up at will. It is only when the people generally, including the young and the students and the intelligentsia—and this latter is very important—are in a state of disaffection, frustration, disillusionment and are alienated from authority (beginning with the Government down to the college authority and local authority), that the conditions for a struggle are ripe. The struggle may break out in violence, or it may take a peaceful form. It need hardly be pointed out that a *peaceful* people's struggle for revolutionary changes would be more acceptable in Gandhi's India than elsewhere, and would not appear in the eyes of the revolutionary activists as a chimera. In either case, leadership and organisation would be necessary to bring out of the revolutionary situation, a revolutionary movement. In the absence of leadership and organisation, the revolutionary situation might end in chaos or imposition of a dictatorship.

August 21

Picking up the thread after a lapse of three days the students' movement gave me an opportunity to turn it into a peaceful people's movement for larger ends : total revolution. Here two points should be made clear. One. I had no specific or direct hand in starting the Bihar movement. Though since the publication of Appeal to the Youth in December 1973 [21] I had specially

21. J.P. wrote this appeal on 11 December 1973 at Acharya Vinoba Bhave's ashram at Paunar. Vinoba endorsed this appeal when it was shown to him by Kusum Deshpande.

concentrated on university students and spoke at the Patna University twice to fairly large student audiences, both times the University Students' Union president presided. I had also spoken at various university centres in U.P., explaining particularly the relevance of my appeal to the forthcoming State Assembly general election. Some of my remarks at these meetings, such as my harking back to the 1942 revolution, undoubtedly stirred the hearts of many students. I had not been to Gujarat immediately before the students' movement there, but some of its prominent leaders claimed to have followed the lead I had given.

Earlier still, I had written and spoken powerfully against political corruption (party, government, administration), suggesting means to check it as well as the need to reform the electoral law and procedure. I had met the PM twice in 1973 specifically to discuss these points, and had come away sorely disappointed. It was then that I had written the article in which I had declared that the people of the country themselves must fight, in peaceful ways of course, for deliverance from the corrupt system under which they were suffering. Apart from corruption, they must also fight hunger, unemployment, inflation, social and economic injustice of many kinds, the futile class system of education, which in the first place left most of their children uneducated and in the second place miseducated the rest. It was in this background of calls for people's and students' action to tackle their problems themselves that both the Gujarat and Bihar students' movements took place.

Be that as it may, it is true that within a couple of months or so, there came to be established a peculiar kind of bond between the student community and me.

Two. When I declared on 5th June 1974 at the Gandhi Maidan (Patna) before a vast audience of students and citizens of Patna—this was after the procession to the Raj Bhavan and presentation of demands to the Rajyapal (State Governor) —that the Bihar movement was no longer a students' movement restricted to the 12 original demands *plus* the few others that had been added since 18th March (the most important of which were the Ministry's ouster and the Assembly's dissolution), but that the movement's or struggle's ultimate aims were nothing

24   PRISON DIARY

less than total revolution, thunderous applause greeted my declaration, thus putting on it the imprimatur of the students' as well as the public's enthusiastic approval. Never at any time was there a breath of opposition to this goal, though there was insistent demand from my students and other colleagues for clarification and elaboration. This I did in many discussions and public speeches, which were published in a pamphlet, entitled *Sampoorna Kranti* (Total Revolution). (I shall briefly elaborate this concept later.) Here suffice it to say that even the limited demands of the students—elimination of corruption, unemployment, 'revolution in education', etc.—were not possible of complete fulfilment without an *all-comprehensive* social revolution, which is what total revolution means in essence. Further, I pointed out (it is implicit in the foregoing sentence) that the mere resignation of a Ministry or the dissolution of an Assembly was not enough, that what was needed was a better political *system*.

Perhaps a little personal digression will be in order here. I had been bitten by the bug of revolution during my high school days. It was then the bug of national revolution, national independence. It was because of this bug that when Gandhiji gave the call for non-cooperation, I too responded. (It was when the non-cooperation movement ebbed that a year and eight months after my non-cooperation, I went to the USA. I wanted to study further and was not willing to go back to the British or aided universities, even to the BHU (Banaras Hindu University), and the *Vidyapeeths* that were established then were hardly in a position to offer facilities for science studies. I was a science student and, further, I had learnt in my high school days from the speeches and writings of Swami Satyadeva Paribrajak that it was possible for students from non-affluent homes to "work" their way up in the American universities, i.e. earn and learn together.) The revolution bug took me to Marxism and through the national freedom movement to democratic socialism and then to Vinobaji's non-violent revolution through love. Before joining Vinobaji I had assured myself through discussions with him that he was concerned not with the mere distribution of land but with a total transformation of man and society, which I described as a double revolution : *social* revolution through *human* revolution.

Such being my ancient preoccupation with revolution (social

revolution after national revolution), and having become satisfied that the gram swarajya movement was not capable of bringing about *ahimsak kranti* (non-violent revolution)—which we had talked about for well-nigh 20 years, from 1954, when I joined Vinobaji, until 1974—I was searching for some other way. Meanwhile I had tried over these years through seminars and conferences, involving in the earlier years some leading lights of the ruling party, to bring about ever so little a change in government policy, planning and a number of other spheres, including electoral reforms. But all these efforts were wasted even in Jawaharlal's times. The leviathan went its own way. The culmination was my two meetings with Mrs Gandhi in 1973 and my being driven to the conclusion of which I have written above. Thus when the Bihar students' movement gathered strength, raised its sights, drew the sympathy and support and, to an extent participation of the people, including the rural people, I considered it was time to see its course towards total revolution. After the meeting of 5th June, the Opposition parties involved in the movement gave their assent—I cannot say to what degree of true conviction and commitment—total revolution came to be accepted overwhelmingly as the goal of the struggle. Slogans and songs about *'Sampoorna kranti ab naaraa hai, bhaavi itihas hamaara hai'* ('Total Revolution is our slogan; Future history belongs to us') reverberated throughout the length and breadth of Bihar, excluding perhaps the Adivasi hinterland. The slogan, if not the song, spread rapidly throughout the Hindi-speaking and Hindi-understanding States of India. Was it the beginning of a nationwide revolutionary movement ? My extensive tours through the country undoubtedly brought an exhilerating mass awakening, but it was doubtful whether it was time yet for the Bihar movement to spread all over the country. First, there seemed to be a lack of proper leadership; second, as the general election approached, the attention of the Opposition came more and more to be turned to the election and to the possibility of exploiting the new awakening to win the election. As I was not only not averse to this but was anxious in the interest of the health of our democracy, to break the Congress monopoly of power at the Centre, I encouraged the Opposition parties to commit themselves to a general people's struggle for comprehen-

sive social change and to use the resulting climate to their advantage at the forthcoming elections. To that end I also tried to
bring them together either into one party or a well-knit front
like the Janata front in Gujarat. My interest in all this, apart
from breaking the Congress monopoly of power, was to be able
to use the Opposition parties' commitment to a people's struggle
to assure that in the event of their succeeding at the Centre and
in the States, the new governments would help and participate
in the revolutionary movement. And with this I turn to elucidate
a vital aspect of the people's struggle, of which I have spoken
much but which, I am afraid, is not fully appreciated yet. This
on some other day; this and why the revolution could not be
brought about by the normal political process.

August 22

The notes on the movement will have to be interrupted today.
There is terrible, terrible news from Bangladesh. It is barbaric.
According to Columbia Broadcasting Correspondent, Richard
Threlkeld, Mujib's wife, his three sons, including the youngest
nine-year-old, two daughters-in-law, two nephews—in all 18 near-
est relations of the late Bangabandhu were killed on the day of
the coup. This barbarity is difficult to understand. Khondkar
Mushtaq Ahmed could not have such cruel hatred or, shall I say,
fear not only of Mujib but also of his wife and children. This takes
us back to the barbaric feudal days when brother killed brother
to seize the crown. Mushtaq Ahmed is talking quite suavely
about the affairs of his country, including friendship for India,
the four 'fundamental principles of State policy': nationalism,
socialism, secularism and democracy. But how can such an evil
deed be reconciled with the attitudes Mr Ahmed is striking? His
taking over supreme martial law powers while still talking of
democracy, I can understand. All dictators talk like this. We have
our own Mrs Gandhi. But why destroy the entire Mujib family?
Was there the fear that if even one member of his family survived
he could become the rallying point for the pro-Mujib force in
the country? Or can it be that the evil deed was performed not

at Mr Ahmed's command, not even by the rebel army leaders'
joint command but on the authority of an army officer, or a
group of officers, who had a serious personal grudge against
Mujib and took their revenge in this ghastly manner ? Only God
knows. Maybe the truth will emerge from the passage of time.
Whatever it be, it is one of the blackest political deeds in recent
history.

Today's papers also publish a Mrs Gandhi-Karanjia interview.
Most of it is the usual stuff : self-righteousness, smugness and the
pose of being the country's saviour. But there are two clear statements, which if taken at their face value give hope for the survival of Indian democracy, may be with its hands and feet tied
and its mouth sealed, but yet breathing and alive. The statements are : (i) there will be no new constitution, the present constitution will remain, though with such alterations as are essential
to perpetuate her rule; (ii) elections will be held, though it is too
early to announce the dates. That is something to be thankful
for. Mrs Gandhi will hold the elections only when she is satisfied
that she has been able to create conditions in which her victory
was assured. Well, that is exactly what the Emergency was proclaimed for. There is no doubt that after Gujarat, the looming
certainty of Opposition unity and the mass awakening as a result
of the movement, she was mortally afraid of a possible electoral
reverse. She must have also been worried about her case in the
Supreme Court. So she fortified her position with amendments to
the Representation of the People Act and the Constitution. Thus
the arrests, the Emergency proclamation, the suppression of the
freedom of the press and of the citizens' fundamental rights of
expression and association (among others) plus the legal and
constitutional amendments add up to one single objective : to
keep Mrs Gandhi safe and warm. (Subsequent events have
proved the last part of my prediction.)

An interesting thing in this interview is that Mrs Gandhi con-
cedes that the former 10 points were not implemented but goes
on to say that if something was not done before, there is no
reason why it should not be done now. We are trying hard, she
said, and there is a 'new spirit of discipline and morale'. Poor
Mohan Dharia and the Young Turks—they have paid heavily
for reminding Mrs Gandhi about the ten points. Now at least

28

they should be happy that their point has been considered. I cannot see that they would be any more optimistic about the implementation of the 20 points than I was in my letter to the PM.[22] irrespective of the new spirit Mrs Gandhi finds in the country.

Now about this new spirit of discipline and morale. I find here too that those in charge of administration are happy that there is more discipline among the employees and subordinates than before. I do not doubt it. But Mrs Gandhi should know that discipline born of fear is nothing to be happy about. A nation cannot be built by fear. It will be a sick nation like a child who being brought up under fear will be a mentally sick adult. I do not know where Mrs Gandhi finds morale. Under fear there can be 'discipline', but not morale. A healthy nation can be built in a climate of freedom. Building up discipline is a two-way process. Our rulers have shown little discipline in recent years, what with corruption, struggle for power, etc. It has been so in every sphere, including the home.

Mr Karanjia has also raised the question of reconciliation. Again Mr Narayan is Mrs Gandhi's main obsession. However, I do not wish to comment on what Mrs Gandhi has said. I should like to record my own thoughts briefly.

The Opposition will answer for itself. But putting myself in its position I ask what reconciliation may mean for it. For Mrs Gandhi it clearly means giving up 'its stand', for in the course of the interview she is reported as saying : '... we have to study the situation a little more before we make any move because I very much doubt whether the Opposition front has given up its stand.' I wish Karanjia had asked her what she meant by that; did she want the Opposition to abdicate and promise full support to Mrs Gandhi and, beyond making some harmless noises in Parliament and on the platform and in the press, behave as good boys like that ideal 'Opposition' party, the CPI ? One wonders.

As I look at it, the primary role of an Opposition in a parliamentary democracy is to endeavour to replace the ruling party

22. The reference is to J P's letter to the Prime Minister dated 21 July, See Appendix 1.

'through the electoral process. Between elections the Opposition works as an Opposition to the Government in parliament and 'through propaganda, constructive work, peaceful demonstrations and other usual democratic means of winning public support, on the one hand; and by putting public pressure on the Government, on the other, the Opposition tries to enlarge its sphere of influence over the electorate as well as bring relief to sections of 'the public who may have been adversely affected by administrative or legislative action.

Normally recourse to civil disobedience is not a part of the Opposition's programme. But on rare occasions, when the government of the day persists in wrongs such as corruption, or in repression such as putting down a legitimate agitation for rectification of crying needs (the Bihar students' movement is an example), the Opposition is compelled to offer civil disobedience.

There are fields—such as social and economic oppression—in which not civil disobedience proper but satyagraha may become necessary. Social workers may be involved, or maybe Opposition groups. Such satyagraha might also turn into civil disobedience against the government, when the latter comes heavily on the side of the oppressors. This has happened again and again in different parts of India where the Congress has been in power. The Opposition can never promise to keep out of such satyagraha.

A last question remains. Can an elected government and legislature be sought to be ousted by civil disobedience, such as in Bihar ? This question has been answered several times and its constitutional admissibility also examined by competent constitutional lawyers. I too have written about it, the last time in my letter to the PM. There is no point in repeating all that again. Two related points, however—and very important points—must be briefly touched upon. One, it is no one's case in what Mrs Gandhi calls the Opposition front that civil disobedience must be the general method, the general pattern, of removing elected governments and legislatures; only in exceptional circumstances can such a course be adopted. Two, even where an elected legislature and government have been ousted or, are sought to be ousted, the new government and legislature must be established only through a general election according to law.

Now, I do not know if Mrs Gandhi wants the Opposition to give up these views, which together constitute what she calls their 'stand'. If, however, she is thinking of such a personal matter as the Opposition demanding her resignation, in terms of the 'Opposition front's' resolution of June 25, 1975 the issue will be dead once the Supreme Court had decided her appeal. Should the verdict be against her, which is unlikely, she has probably some ordinance ready to render it null and void. In that case, the Opposition is not likely to give up its demand for her resignation, which would be perfectly justified. But there is no possibility of the Opposition mounting a civil disobedience movement to that end. Placed as the Opposition is today it will, most probably, girt its loins to prepare for the next elections, which Mrs Gandhi promises at some future date convenient to her.

That I think will be the Opposition's stand, of which I shall fully approve. What will be my stand ? I too shall put my heart and soul into the election and fight it shoulder to shoulder with the Opposition. I have no desire to offer myself as a candidate or to join any party or front. But I shall go all out to see that the Opposition wins. So much of this country's future depends upon it that it would be a political crime to shirk this responsibility at this time.

What else ? What about my theory of a people's movement and its role in total revolution ? This is the point I am centrally concerned with in the notes that I am writing and herein will my views be found.

August 23

*(Notes on the movement continued. Yesterday's note
on Karanjia's interview should also be taken to be a
part of the Notes.)*

Since independence, full 28 years now, there has been no real change in the social, economic and political structure of our society. Zamindari is abolished, land reform laws have been passed, untouchability has been legally prohibited, and so on. But the village in most parts of India is still in the grip of the higher castes and the bigger and the medium landowners. The small and the marginal landowners and the landless, the backward classes and the Harijans—these form the majority in most villages in most States, perhaps in nine-tenths of India. Yet their position continues to be miserable, Harijans are still burnt alive. The Adivasis are still the most backward section, barring the Harijans. And the money-lenders (who include many landowners and the shopkeepers, maybe petty themselves) mercilessly cheat and exploit the Adivasis, who in Bihar call the plainsmen *dikku*.[23]

Some industries, banks, life insurance have been nationalised. Railways were nationalised long ago. New large public sector industries have been established. But all this adds up to state capitalism and inefficiency, waste and corruption. State capitalism means more power to the state, mainly the state bureaucracy or what Galbraith aptly calls the 'public bureaucracy'. There is no element or trait of socialism in all this. The working class and the public or, let us say, the people have no place in all this except as workers or consumers. There is no 'economic democracy' which is so much talked about, neither even industrial democracy. This does not mean that I am opposed to socialism. It is only because I am so deeply concerned about socialism that I am pointing all this out. It is a pity that our socialists very largely equate socialism with nationalisation.

The educational system in spite of several committees and commissions remains *basically* what it was during British rule : class education designed as an escalator to reach the top. There is so much to say about this, but this is not the place. Here I am trying only to show that the structure of society has remained unchanged through the years since independence.

The customs, manners, beliefs, superstitions, all these remain much the same for the masses. Even among the classes the change is superficial in most parts.

Since independence there has been a steady decline in political, public and business morality.

If we take social and economic development, the picture is frightful. The population growth goes racing forward. Poverty is also growing : more than 40 per cent of the people are below the

23. 'Outsider', a term used by the Adivasis for the plainsmen.

poverty line. The barest necessities such as drinking water, man-worthy and not cattle-worthy housing, medical care, apart from food and clothing, are not available. Schools are few and the teaching is bad. The papers say today that Bihar is the richest state in the country in minerals. Bihar also has good land and perennial rivers. Why then is Bihar the poorest state in India ? Well, one could go on adding to the list.

The question is, can the picture be fundamentally altered through the ordinary democratic process ? Even if the Opposition wins, will the picture change ? I fear, no. Laws will be passed and applied, moneys will be spent—even if all this is done, pos-sibly without corruption creeping in, will the structure, the system, the 'order' of our society change ? I think, no. Why ?

Before I answer let me elucidate what I mean by a few exam-ples. Take the marriage customs, particularly the *tilak* and *dahez* system, prevalent in Bihar, Bengal, U.P. and some other States. This evil has been sought to be corrected by law, but the law has been a dead letter. Meanwhile the disease is growing fast, ruin-ing many families and ruining the lives of many girls. Castes that had till the other day been free of this evil are rapidly falling a prey to it, because what is a social evil appears to them to be a status symbol. There is no remedy but a vigorous social move-ment, a peaceful struggle against the evil. Likewise, the implemen-tation of land reforms, homestead tenancy legislation, removal of corruption in the administration, etc. All this requires a mass awakening and a mass struggle. The youth, including the students, must naturally be in the vanguard.

August 23

The question is even larger. It is how to bring about a systemic change in society; i.e. how to bring about what I have called a total revolution : revolution in every sphere and aspect of society. The question becomes harder to answer when it is added that the total revolution has to be peacefully brought about without impairing the democratic structure of society and affecting the democratic way of life of the people. Put in this way, even the most legalistic and constitutionalist democrat would agree that all this could never be accomplished if the functioning of democracy were restricted to elections, legislation, planning and administrative execution. There must also be people's direct action. This action would almost certainly comprise, among other forms, civil disobedience, peaceful resistance, non-cooperation—in short, satyagraha in its widest sense. One of the unstated implications of such satyagraha would be self-change; that is to say, those wanting a change must also change themselves before launching any kind of action.

I recall Chandrashekhar several times asking me what the Bihar movement, or any other such movement, would achieve if it were only to replace the Congress government with a government of the Opposition. Will that government be any better ? It was a valid question, which the Opposition parties should ponder. Their performance in 1967 was certainly a great disappointment.

My answer to Chandrashekhar used to be that the movement's aim was not only to change the government in Bihar, but much more which I had "capsuled" (if I may coin this word) in the term revolution. The movement would go on, which in itself would be a powerful guarantee of the Opposition government always being on its toes, and that it would go on faster and smoother because the new government would give its full co-operation. In fact, a point to stress here is—and this I have done so often in the course of the Bihar movement—that had the Bihar government at the outset decided to cooperate with the students in examining and attempting seriously to solve the problems they had highlighted in their twelve demands, there would have been no question of the Bihar students' movement wanting to remove the Bihar government. As is well known by now, the demand for the removal of the Ministry and the Assembly came much later as a result of the violence, repression and lies let loose by the then Bihar government.

The upshot of what I have been saying is that the people's movement of the type I am visualising here can proceed either in cooperation or in confrontation with the government concerned. I enunciated this principle clearly for the first time in my speech at the civic reception at Poona (on 23rd January

1975). But this was not a thought that had suddenly dawned upon me at the reception. It had always been present in my mind and I am sure I had spoken several times before about it. But because of the fact that the Poona Municipal Corporation, though in the hands of the Opposition with a Socialist Mayor, had ruling Congress members too within its fold and they too had voted for my reception, I thought it necessary to enunciate that principle as clearly as possible. For the Poona press it was something new and they highlighted it and it was very well reported in the national press. That is why it was thought at that time that I had made a new departure. Indeed, it appeared like that to some Opposition leaders in Bihar too. But the very procedure laid down for the starting of a movement implicitly accepted this position. First, a number of demands that are most important for the people are drawn up and they are presented to the Chief Minister. If upon that the Chief Minister were to say, "Well, all right let us sit together and work this out; I am prepared to cooperate with you in solving these problems and removing these evils'—corruption in the Ministry, for instance—the struggle (for it still remains a struggle—a struggle not against the Government but against certain evils and for certain changes and objectives) takes the course of cooperation. So far, not a single Congress government has chosen to follow this course. More often, there is no reply at all or if there is, it is evasive and beside the point.

August 27

Another interruption today in these Notes. When I wrote to Prabha and Sheela [24] yesterday I had no idea that the floods in Patna were so terrible. This morning's *Hindustan Times* gives harrowing details. I feel so miserable and helpless sitting here idly when my people there are in the grip of such an unprecedented catastrophe. The poor and lower middle class people

24. Mrs Prabha Chowdhary and Mrs Sheela Rukhaiyar are workers of the Mahila Charkha Samiti.

must be undergoing hell. Those who lived in single-storey tiled or even *pucca* buildings must have lost their all. Where could they remove their belongings ? I do not know what is happening in the low-level Mahila Charkha Samiti. The water there must be six to eight feet deep. Common people in the city must be starving. And what about drinking water ? That must be even a more serious problem than food. Most people must be drinking the contaminated flood water. I do not know what kind of relief operations there are. I doubt the Bihar government's ability to do much in such crisis. The Army and the Air Force might be of more help.

I have been thinking whether I should ask for a month's or even a fortnight's release on parole to organise popular relief. With all communications in chaos the work would be difficult. But I could mobilise the youth from the non-flood areas and also mobilise help from other States. Yes, as I think more about it, much could be done. All the popular leaders of the State are in jail. Most of the Congress leaders are corrupt and easy-going. The Bihar administration is also not so efficient. Well, I shall decide by this afternoon whether to request for parole or not. I recall that at the time of the great earthquake in 1934,[25] the British released Rajen Babu from the Hazaribagh jail—not on any request from him but on their own. But Mrs Gandhi is not so human or weak, if you will, as the British imperialists !

Have decided now to send the following message to the PM through the DC (Deputy Commissioner, Chandigarh) :

Prime Minister
New Delhi

Feel deeply distressed at reports of Patna and Bihar floods. Never in known history had Patna suffered thus. Feel thoroughly miserable and helpless sitting idly here. Pray for a month's release on parole so that I may mobilise people's help from within and without the State and organise popular relief in cooperation with State and Central governments. Even if floods

25. The earthquake in Bihar on 15th January 1934 damaged all buildings in an area of about 6,000 sq. miles and killed nearly 10,000 persons. Darbhanga, Champaran and Muzaffarpur were the worse hit.

recede there would remain colossal work to be done. At the time of the Great Bihar Earthquake of 1934 the British had released Rajen Babu from the Hazaribagh jail for similar work. Request urgent attention and action.

—JAYAPRAKASH

I have requested this message to be communicated by telephone or express wire.

August 28

It is too early to expect any reply from Delhi. Most probably nothing is going to happen. It is a pity, because the occasion and my request give her a very good opportunity to unhook herself from a position that she is finding so hard to justify to honest and impartial Indian and world opinion. (The only way she can do so is by magnifying hundredfold the danger of internal disturbance.) This convinces no one. Assuming that she does want to get out of the mess she has got herself in (not to speak of the mess in which she has plunged the country), she can find a way out by drawing a parallel with what happened at the time of the Bihar earthquake of 1934. It will be recalled that after the failure of the Round Table Conference and Gandhiji's return, the British government launched an offensive and even as the Working Committee was meeting at Mani Bhawan in Gamdevi, Bombay, Jawaharlal was arrested at Manekpur, I believe, as he was travelling from Allahabad (Chheoki) to Bombay by the Bombay Mail. I happened to be travelling with him—at that time I was working in the AICC office at Swaraj Bhawan. (Khan Abdul Ghaffar Khan had already been arrested in Peshawar.) There was a round-up of Congress leaders throughout the country. Gandhiji was also arrested and imprisoned in Yervada. In reaction, the civil disobedience movement, suspended as a result of the Gandhi-Irwin Pact, was resumed. This was in January 1933.

In early 1934 this movement was formally still on, but instead of mass civil disobedience there was civil disobedience by secretly recruited persons who on certain announced days came out into the open and civilly broke the law in accordance with programmes drawn up by underground State or district Congress Committees which were really civil disobedience committees. So, when Rajen Babu was released—a few months before the expiry of the term—the civil disobedience had not yet been called off formally. Because with Working Committee members still in jail, the movement could not be officially called off. But at the time of natural catastrophe of the dimensions of the Great Earthquake, Rajen Babu or no other Congress leader of Bihar could think of carrying on the movement. Their primary and urgent duty was to put themselves at the service of the stricken people. A relief committee had already been formed, but with Rajen Babu in command the entire situation was electrified. Vast relief operations were soon put in motion and I remember that Rajen Babu's relief fund followed closely at the heels of the Viceroy's relief fund. Soon there was a general jail delivery in Bihar. Gandhiji himself came to the State to help. Jawaharlal also, Jamnalalji [26] and many other all-India leaders played some part in the relief operations. Professor J. C. Kumarappa [27] took charge of the accounts section. And so on. Thus without anybody formally withdrawing the movement, the great calamity having attracted and absorbed all the attention and energies of the national leaders, the civil disobedience programme came to an honourable end. The British government too accepted the position and the special repressive laws were withdrawn or allowed to lapse. All prisoners too were released within a few months, either having served their terms or as part of policy.

Should Mrs Gandhi be anxious to normalise the situation, the Bihar floods give her an opportunity. If I am released on parole or otherwise, my first duty would be to put myself and all my friends and co-workers in Bihar and other States to the service of the people. To think of a movement or struggle at this time would be to mock the unprecedented misery of the people. The Bihar movement would thus naturally be put aside. I have offered in my message to the PM that I would work in cooperation with the State and Central governments. That should put her fears

26. The late Jamnalal Bajaj, Gandhian industrialist and for many years Treasurer of the Congress Party.
27. A Gandhian economist, now dead.

at rest. Under these conditions a general jail delivery of those connected with the movement should be a logical step. They shall all be mobilised for relief work. I shall invite all-India leaders too to Bihar to help us. The sweeping all-India arrests were thoroughly unjustified, and with our attention and energies turned to relief work there should be no fear in Mrs Gandhi's mind about the natural catastrophe being utilised by me for the movement. Thus the tension in the country would be eased and democracy restored and 'normalcy', of which Mrs Gandhi talks so much, re-established.

The question is, has Mrs Gandhi enough imagination to see all this ? But perhaps a deeper question is, does Mrs Gandhi want democracy and normalcy to return ? From all that she has been doing since 1971 at least, it appears that she is afraid of democracy because then she is not sure if she would remain in power. And Mrs Gandhi must remain in power, whatever the cost ! Therefore, I am sure there will be no reply from her, or if there is, it will be a negative one. Let it be so. Perhaps it is better that way. Let the people see how far down she can descend. The ultimate victory will be the people's.

It occurs to me that there might also be in Mrs Gandhi's mind a selfish thought which may prevent her from taking steps to normalise the situation in Bihar in view of the terrible catastrophe. She might think that with Jayaprakash and all the Opposition and many Sarvodaya leaders and workers of Bihar being out of the way, the entire credit for saving Bihar from the Great calamity would go to her and her party and government in Bihar and at the Centre. Well, she might think so, but I am sure that as soon as the Army and Air Force hand back the relief operations to the civil powers, all the inefficiency and corruption of the Bihar Government and administration and of the Bihar Congressmen will come into play. The harvest of all this will not be so pleasant as Mrs Gandhi expects. The experience of the Bihar famine of 1966-67 may be recalled. Whatever the faults of the Coalition Government which took power in March 1967, it certainly set a better record in relief work than the Congress Government had done. However, let me hope for the sake of the people of Bihar that the Bihar Government and Congress will give a better account of themselves this time. If the credit goes to them and Mrs Gandhi, they would deserve it and no one would mind it.

N.B. Lest what I have written above about all thought of the 'movement or struggle' being set aside in Bihar in order to concentrate on relief work should appear as a subconscious or even a conscious but concealed ruse to regain freedom from detention, I should record here that this is exactly how I have reacted to every situation of the kind facing Bihar now. During the Bihar famine of 1966-67 this is exactly what I did. All Sarvodaya work in the affected districts was suspended, Sarvodaya workers from other districts were withdrawn and posted to the affected areas, even all-India Sarvodaya leaders were invited and involved, Siddharaj Dhaddha being the chief among them.

There was some difference of opinion among Sarvodaya workers at that time, but by and large it received overwhelming support. Relief work through gram sabhas was emphasised by Ram Murtiji [28] and endorsed by Vinobaji, but unfortunately there were hardly a dozen villages which had a functioning gram sabha that could handle a big job like relief. The tendency in the villages generally was for the better-off sections to ensure that they got the lion's share of the relief benefits : I had no objection to relief being administered through gram sabhas—in fact I whole-heartedly wished it—but in view of the vast scale of relief operations on which the BRC [29] was working it was just impossible, barring very rare exceptions, to rely on the gram sabhas. Again, in the year 1961 when parts of Monghyr district— Lakhisarai, Kharagpur and the surrounding areas, I believe— which never had been stricken by floods were suddenly overtaken by unprecedented floods caused by excessive rain, particularly in the hills, I had the same policy followed.

P. S. Perhaps the civil disobedience movement did not quietly pass into desuetude as I have noted above, or rather while it did so, in fact, it was also *formally* withdrawn at an AICC meeting in Patna, perhaps in May 1934. 'We' (the Congress Socialists) had opposed it, but the resolution was, of course, passed and a constructive programme was adopted. It was at that same time that I had called on behalf of the Bihar Socialist Party a

28. Acharya Ram Murti, prominent Sarvodya worker and intellectual.
29. Bihar Relief Committee set up by J P to fight the unprecedented drought and famine in Bihar in 1967.

conference of Congressmen believing in socialism. Acharya Narendra Deva presided and Professor Abdul Bari was Chairman of the Reception Committee. The Conference met in the Anjuman Islamia Hall and appointed me Organising Secretary to organise an all-India party of socialist Congressmen within the Indian National Congress. Looking back, it seems wrong to have decided to form a party with its policy and programme, membership, constitution and rules. A loose group or bloc would have been better and constitutionally valid. The High Command did not take any action because the genuineness, sincerity and devotion to the cause of independence of the Congress Socialists was beyond question.

August 30

Pages 33-34 show how my concept of struggle need not inevitably include a struggle against the government of the State. It is up to the Government concerned to decide what policy it will follow: that of cooperation or of confrontation. The question is, why have the Congress governments, wherever faced with a people's charter of demands, never found it possible to adopt the path of cooperation ? The answer, as I indicated in my letter to the PM, lies in the corruption among Congress Ministers. Mrs Gandhi's own conduct in collecting crores of rupees from rich businessmen for party and election management is a piece of political corruption that has completely destroyed the moral susceptibilities of most power-seeking Congressmen. Party and election funds were collected in Jawaharlal's time also, in Shri Babu's [30] time also (to speak only of Bihar, but it was done everywhere), but the scale of operations was comparatively small and most of the money was accounted for. In any case, it never happened that only Jawaharlal knew how much was collected; others also like Sardar or S. K. Patil knew it. Nor were business bargains struck in the process so shamelessly corrupt as those of which one has heard in Mrs Gandhi's time.

30. Shri Krishna Sinha, first Chief Minister of Bihar, who was popularly known as Shri Babu.

Be that as it may, corruption being the focal point of the recent students' and people's movements, and the Congress Ministries in the States or at the Centre not being prepared to face the issue, they could not but adopt the consistently hostile attitude they have adopted to the movement. There was also perhaps a stronger reason, though it was not visible. When the Congress found that the movement was not going to be satisfied with superficial remedies but that it was also aiming to bring about basic fundamental changes in society, including basic political changes—in short, a total revolution—it was too much for it to stomach. Opposition from the Government was natural, through raising a cloud of dust about 'danger to democracy', danger of 'internal disturbance', etc.

The question is, will the Opposition parties behave differently? That is yet to be seen. But having once joined the movement, no doubt to exploit it for party and election purposes (which is in the very nature of political parties), they find themselves not only committed to the final goal of total revolution but also being radicalised in the process of the struggle. Even about exploiting the movement for party ends, I cannot deny that they have tried to do so in Bihar—the better organised and disciplined the party, the more guilty it has been. But in the total picture, it will not be wrong to say that the interests of the struggle have been generally placed above the interests of the party. The only exceptions are places where only one party holds sway and the non-party forces among students, citizens and the local Sarvodaya workers are weak; the party in question has in that case identified its party interests with the interests of the struggle. It was precisely with a view to strengthening the non-party forces that I had been busy organising a new volunteer force of non-party youths and students called Chhatra-Yuva Sangharsha Vahini. A big rally of these youths was to be held and addressed by me at Patna on the day of my arrest, 26th June 1975.

There is one difficulty about this concept of peaceful social or total revolution. Can the necessary psychological climate of struggle be created at will ? If not, the struggle of this concept is as unlikely to get off the ground as Vinobaji's movement for gram swarajya. True, the pre-conditions for a social struggle (using the term social in its widest sense) are always present in poverty, unemployment, mis-education, etc. But still there is need for a spark to kindle the fires of struggle, to set alight the dry tinder-box of Indian society.

There is another minor difficulty too. That is about the non-Congress and non-CPI Opposition parties. Unless a struggle involves struggle against the Congress government they will not feel attracted towards it, because in that case it hardly promises any dividends. Indeed, they might fear that if the struggle is against the vested interests (as it must to have any meaning), their participation in it might adversely affect their electoral chances. This may not be true of some of the left parties, however.

Is there an answer to these difficulties ? No, if we start writing on a clean slate. The future struggle must be related to the past struggle and pick up the thread where it had been dropped when the arrests were made and the Emergency was clamped down. The longer the fighters are kept in prison, the better would it be for resumption of the struggle. It is difficult at this stage to guess when, if at all, the general elections to the Lok Sabha and the Vidhan Sabhas will be held. 'If at all' in the preceding sentence is perhaps a wrong presumption. In her statements and interviews in the last two months Mrs Gandhi has repeatedly committed herself to holding elections. When, is the question. From her point of view the right time will be when the Oppostion is sufficiently demoralised and the people won over by her 20-point programme and sugared words and announcement of dazzling policies—which like fireworks will dazzle for a moment, then leave everything behind just as it was before. Whenever that moment comes for Mrs Gandhi, the election dates will be announced and the detenus released. With all the Opposition leaders and other detenus remaining in jail, the election would be an utter farce. It would be difficult for Mrs Gandhi to persuade public opinion in India and abroad, particularly in the West, that elections under such conditions could ever be an exercise in democracy. Not even the British dared to do that in India.

Now, whatever happens in other States, the Congress has no chance in Bihar in a free and fair election. Then, with a pro-struggle government established, the struggle would be resumed again. (By the way, this could be done in Gujarat today, but there seems to be no one there to relate the Navanirman movement to the present most favourable political situation in that State.) However, it may be Bihar's opportunity and good fortune to show how a society could be changed with the active cooperation between the people and the government.

Here I must comment on the usual talk of 'cooperation of the people', 'participation of the people', etc. Mrs Gandhi is also indulging a great deal in such talk and Mr Borooah—yes, the inevitable Mr Borooah—is busy setting up committees of the people to do this. In the heyday of Community Development this was common claptrap. But we who were working at the ground level then—in the villages—discovered what all that meant. It did not mean any initiative on the part of the people; it only meant that the better-off people in the villages drained off everything or almost everything that the development pipeline was bringing to the people.

The case I am visualising for Bihar would be different. The struggle committees, the *janata sarkars* would pick up the thread where it was broken and beginning with the items of the movement's programme as it stood at that moment, they would forge ahead towards the goal of total revolution, the State government helping where its help was needed and taking help where it needed help itself. It is an exciting picture and I do pray to God to be spared to play such part as I may in this historic process.

What about other States ? Well, I think Bihar's example would provide the stimulus and the movement—struggle and reconstruction, confrontation and cooperation—would spread.

August 31

Dear Mr. Devasahayam,[31]

I have been thinking of my request to the PM about being released on parole. It seems to me that the possibility of my using the opportunity for political purposes might weigh on the PM's mind and make it difficult for her to take a positive deci-

31. Mr M. G. Devasahayam, Deputy Commissioner of Chandigarh.

sion. Apprehending this, I hereby request you to have it conveyed to the PM as soon as possible that there need be no apprehension at all on this score. I would consider it immoral and impolitic to exploit the period of freedom allowed to me for any political purpose. Indeed to talk of politics at this time would be to mock the miseries and sufferings of the people. No one with a grain of human sympathy would ever think of doing such a thing.

I have just re-read the draft of my message to the PM. (By the way, it was written in a sort of telegraphic language so that it could be communicated by telephone or wire.) On re-reading the message I find that assurance that I would confine myself to relief work alone is already implicit in it. It is made somewhat explicit by the words 'in cooperation with the State and Central governments'.

I shall be grateful if you have this clarification conveyed to Delhi so that it reaches the PM before she takes a decision on my request.

Yours Sincerely,
JAYAPRAKASH NARAYAN

(Notes continued) **August 31**

What I wrote yesterday may be only one way a movement for total change might spread to other States. But there is another and more probable way perhaps. As the Gujarat and Bihar movements showed, it might grow out of a comparatively minor agitation and then spread like wildfire. In Gujarat it began with agitation against a students' hostel warden and rapidly grew, forcing Mrs Gandhi and the Central government to compel the Gujarat Ministry to resign and finally dissolve the Assembly. Unfortunately, there was no one in Gujarat who could have carried forward the movement until at least its other aims had been achieved; removal of corruption, educational reform, solution of the problem of unemployment. For the students of Gujarat it was a dazzling victory and no one can blame them for being dazzled by their success. That success and Morarjibhai's fast led to elections being held and the victory of the Janata Front. This too was a great outcome of that struggle. But, like Chandrashekhar, historians in the future might ask: 'What was it all for? If that was all, why could they not wait until the next election?' This is one of Mrs Gandhi's favourite propaganda themes.

Well, this question and this line of propaganda would have been quite valid had the Gujarat movement ended merely in replacing the Congress with the Janata Front in power. Superficially, it appears like this. But on deeper understanding the conclusion becomes inescapable that the Gujarat movement was a path-finder in India's march towards democracy, withal parliamentary democracy, in which the demos, the people, are not mere passive agents but are active, demanding and in the end commanding. The Gujarat movement established for the first time in India the primacy of the people, going over the heads of organised parties and asserting their will. True, it were the students and the youths who seemed to be manning the battle-front, but without the support of the people behind them they could not have won. And the reason why the people backed the students was that the latter articulated the people's own grievances, desires and aims (no matter how vaguely formulated). India and Indian democracy will never be the same after the Gujarat movement. Having said all this, I must again repeat that it was a pity (a) the Gujarat movement ended with the dissolution of the Assembly, and (b) no one is trying to utilise a friendly and responsive government to re-start a revolutionary movement—call it a Nava-Navaniraman movement or whatever—that could present an example of how there could be cooperation in place of confrontation in bringing about a total revolution in society.

I seem to have digressed from the main point I set out to make at the beginning. It is simply this that no one can tell after Gujarat and Bihar what little spark anywhere may lead to a revolutionary movement in a State or in any area. The preconditions being present everywhere as in the two examples, it can begin and spread anywhere in the country. This is another, and a quite unpredictable manner in which a Bihar-type movement may develop in other parts of India.

46

In one of her statements Mrs Gandhi, speaking obliquely about me and my colleagues in the movement, said that for us the students could do no wrong; they could burn down buses, commit other kinds of violence and scenes of rowdyism, but (for us) they were sacred, nothing could be said against them, etc., etc. Now, I had decided not to comment any more on Mrs Gandhi's sayings, but on this point I must say something because the students have played such a vital role in both the Gujarat and Bihar movements and they are likely to play a greater part in the future. In Gujarat there is no doubt that violence was committed against both property and person. But this was done by a small section of the students who were either anxious to show how militant they were or were under the influence of a political party that was not committed to peaceful methods. In most cases of violence police provocation sometimes in extreme and indecent forms, was the spark. Be that as it may, the bulk of the students participating in the Gujarat movement believed in and adhered to peaceful methods. Interestingly, one of the most prominent leaders of the Navanirman Samiti, who was the most vocal advocate of violence, has now joined Mrs Gandhi's party.

As for Bihar, it has been admitted even in official quarters that but for my intervention and active guidance there would have been widespread violence by the students. Mrs Gandhi knows the facts but she has not the honesty to give the Devil his due. She was maligning me when she said that the students could burn and destroy, but I (referring to me indirectly as she mostly does) never condemned their action. This is a lie. To give only one example, when the Satyagrahis in Bihar in the early days were trying by entreaty and lying in their path to prevent the MLAs from entering the Assembly, and one day when some MLAs were manhandled by the Satyagrahis, resulting in someone's shirt being torn, I publicly condemned it and wrote to the Speaker, Mr Harinath Mishra, expressing my sorrow and requesting him to convey my deep regrets and apologies to the MLAs concerned. (The Speaker was kind enough to read out my letter in the Assembly.) There were also some other occasions when, I had condemned violence and urged strict adherence to peaceful methods. When a constable was killed—he himself was innocent—by a violent mob which had been unnecessarily provoked, not only did I condemn the act but also publicly apologised to the Bihar Police, sent my condolences to his widow as well as a sum of Rs. 5,000. No, the Bihar movement or any other Bihar-type movement does not think and will never think that the students or, for that matter, anyone else is above the law and could do what he liked. Where a particular law had to be disobeyed, it had to be done in an organised and peaceful manner. No one in the movement was or will ever be allowed to take the law in his own hands.

So much for violence, and the students in the movement. But the important thing for Mrs Gandhi is to find out why university students burn buses and commit similar other acts. It is one of the most important questions before the country. Studies on student unrest do not give all the answers. But it is possible to formulate a policy on the basis of the answers available. But who will have the courage to put this policy into practice ? The policy will cover not only the educational field but also many other fields, such as economic and social development, their direction, and the restructuring of the class organisation of society. I am afraid the middle classes, from whom most politicians, bureaucrats, teachers, businessmen, professionals, and the like come, will, on one specious pretext or another, block any revolutionary change either in the educational system or the socio-economic, political, cultural sphere. Maybe, some day in these Notes I shall elaborate this point.

Under the Emergency there may be no buses being burnt today and Mrs Gandhi might think she has solved the problem of student unrest, indiscipline and violence. But if the Emergency lasts longer, Mrs Gandhi may be faced with a most unexpected explosion.

Earlier in these Notes (see entry for July 21) I have mentioned the two drops of essence that I wanted to distil out of all the clang and clamour of the Bihar movement. If the objectives of the Bihar type of people's movement were to be listed, the two objectives stated in the aforesaid Notes would be the first to be included. The other objective would be to start a revolutionary movement of total change in society with the participation of the people, with the youth and students in the forefront perhaps, either with the cooperation of the government or in confrontation with it. The role of political parties will have to be discussed. The agents of change, the Vanguard; the role of idealistic youth; the need for a comprehensive struggle for change : these points will have to be clearly elaborated. I have noted them down here merely as an aid to memory. This has to be elaborated in the next few days.

September 4

The letter to the P M [32] has not gone yet. I have not even bothered to make the final draft. I am waiting for a response from Delhi.

Some sort of response has come today. Mr Vorah,[33] Additional Secretary, Food and Agriculture Ministry, Delhi, came this afternoon. He was advised to see me by Professor P. N. Dhar. Mr Vorah told me how he went to Patna and all that he found there and did. The most extraordinary thing I learnt from him was how the CM,[34] CS [35] and other ministers and officers, except

32. See Appendix 2. This letter was drafted on September 2, but was not sent to the Prime Minister.
33. Mr B. B. Vorah, an expert on problems of soil and water conservation in India.
34. Chief Minister.
35. Chief Secretary.

the Commissioner, Patna and the DM, were in a 'trauma' and had hardly moved to do anything. The CM was marooned in his house, but had not thought of getting out by boat or by wading through the flood waters. Mr Vorah, like a senior officer, was very circumspect and restrained about it all. It was clear from his report that had not the Central government moved in the matter and made use of the Air Force and taken steps to activise the State government, the latter would have done little until the situation had improved enough by the flood waters receding. In all this Mr Vorah's part seems to have been outstanding.

Listening to all that Mr. Vorah said, I wondered why he had been sent to me. Again, he was circumspect but it was clear that Professor Dhar wanted to find out what my reaction was. Sensing this, I told Mr Vorah when he had finished, that what I had heard from him made me still more eager and anxious to be with the stricken people of Patna and Bihar in order to serve them to the best of my ability. I told him that people must be helped to help themselves and for that they must be awakened from *their* trauma and organised. This, the Government, the Congress leaders, I am afraid, could not do—this too I told Mr Vorah. Bihar's misfortune is a national misfortune and a national effort has to be made. If I were free I could mobilise volunteers from the rest of the country, raise funds, etc. I told him that one rupee spent by an honest voluntary relief body was equal to ten spent by the government. So I begged the Government of India or, rather, the PM to give serious and sympathetic thought to my earlier request.

I told Mr Vorah another thing which was relevant to this problem though he was uneasy about discussing any political aspect of the matter. I told him to tell Professor Dhar from me that this was a good time to review the entire policy that had been followed in the name of the Emergency. I assured him that there could be no question of anyone exploiting this unprecedented calamity for political ends. Political exploitation of the Bihar situation would be a mockery of the sufferings of the people.

An interesting and encouraging thing that I found was that Mr Vorah had studied the problem of water management, annual washing off of the fertile top soil into the sea and other related problems. He seemed very keen about something serious and long-term being done about it, and added that what was needed was political will. I told him I could not agree more with him. In Bihar, I have noticed that during every great natural calamity, like the great famine of 1966-67, there was a lot of talk of long-term solutions, of war-footing operations, but once the calamity was over, the sordid selfish game of politics started. What I did not tell him was I wondered if it would be any different this time.

Mr Vorah's estimate was that a comprehensive use of water management and land management would cost about Rs. 50 thousand crore—a large sum for a poor country. But if the losses from natural calamities are added up Rs. 50 thousand crore might already have been lost since independence. During the Bihar famine the, loss was estimated at Rs 600 crore. The Bihar CM estimates this year's flood losses at Rs 500 crore, of which Patna's share is Rs 100 crore.

Incidentally, here is the answer to the question often asked (among others by me too) why Bihar so richly endowed by nature is the poorest State in India. This is certainly the most important reason. Within a decade, counting from 1966, Bihar has suffered a loss of Rs 1100 crore—and that too from only two calamities, the famine and this year's floods. Besides, every year some part or another of the State has suffered either from drought or floods.

September 5

Tapan Dasgupta has a short piece of reporting from Patna in today's *Hindustan Times*. What a grim, frightful picture has he drawn! What complete lack of leadership or initiative on the part of the Bihar Ministry and Mrs Gandhi's wonderful party in the State! It seems there was complete paralysis on their part on the 25th, 26th, 27th—the worst days. As Mr Vorah said yesterday, the CM and the others had an attack of trauma, from which they hardly recovered until the Central government took the initiative. The very first meeting held in Patna, 'called' by the CM, of the principal officers of the State government, the Electricity Board Chief, the DS, Railways, the Air Force and Army leaders was at Mr Vorah's initiative! However, it gladdens one's heart to know that all citizens were not suffering from trauma, that some ordinary folks *had* shown initiative and inventiveness. And who is this young man Suresh? He must be a remarkably brave, resourceful and humane person. According to Tapan, his was the first relief enterprise, wading through chest-deep water with biscuits and other things. God knows there must have been scores of such young men or even older men and women in other areas showing initiative in different ways. Ah, how my heart yearns to be in Patna and in Bihar at this moment! If God wills, I shall be there.

September 5

The Egypt-Israeli agreement has been signed by two parties at Geneva. Russia, as expected, declined to send a representative, so the US also stayed away.

Dr Kissinger deserves the grateful thanks of humanity for bringing about some advance—important only in holding the promise of a more solid and comprehensive agreement not only between these two nations but also comprehending that intrepid and brave patriot, Arafat, and then, naturally, Syria too. President Sadat is surely a very wise and far-seeing statesman. It must have taken great courage to do what he has done. I hope he lives until the final peace agreement is concluded and no assassin succeeds in cutting short the newly-born hope of a peaceful and prosperous West Asia. Not only West Asia but the world.

It is heartening to learn that Sadat is anxious to turn his attention to the Golan heights question which is so vital for Syria and the Palestinians. But they must recognize that Israel has a right to exist and to live within secure and guaranteed borders. They must also learn that terror and war cannot ever be a lasting solution, no matter who wins. And they must remember that a serious war in West Asia must inextricably entangle the two superpowers, which might mean the end of the world, or at least of the world as it is and is promising to be. Perhaps it is here that there lies safety for humanity. When faced with the ultimate choice of war or peace between them, they must withdraw from the brink and choose peace, not out of love for humanity but for their own existence upon this earth. So the initiative very appropriately lies in the hands of that wisest and bravest of recent Arab leaders, including Nasser, President Anwar Sadat. One hopes that Saudi Arabia, solid and authoritative and also balanced, will be on Sadat's side and on the side of a just and lasting peace.

Russia is perhaps worried about the balance of power in West Asia. Russia is a great country with a great stake in peace. As the Arab-Israeli conflict is slowly resolved, both America and Russia will find that Arab nationalism will not brook anyone's interference in their affairs. The Russians have a reliable agent in every country, the local communist party. But I do not see any great future for any of these parties, because whenever there is a conflict in the present world system between genuine *nationalism* and communism with extra-territorial patriotism, communism will come the loser, unless Russia is able to deploy her armies in these countries as she has been doing in Eastern Europe. But if Russia is ever immature enough to do such a thing, she will be face to face with American power. No, I do not think that is a possible course to follow for either America or Russia. The world has shrunken so, and these superpowers sit so astride the earth, that for them the balance of power is no longer regional, as in the old days of European imperialism. For them it is really a world balance of power. And there, though in fighting capacity both seem to be equal, Russia has to catch up with America in production, both agricultural and industrial and with the necessary *technology* for that. For Russia that means the gut of the balance of power with America.

Coming back to communism in West Asia, the Russian brand will have to compete with the Chinese and this may be a needling matter for the Russian giant. The Chinese giant, no rival in military and economic power, may become quite a serious rival in the war for winning men's minds and hearts. But this will not affect seriously the balance of power in West Asia as the term is usually understood. Or so it seems to me.

September 5

Tarkunde has very kindly sent me again (earlier he had sent me the Bhagvadgita, 2 volumes of the Upanishads and a good book on the latter by Swami Ranganathananda) four books by Rajni Kothari and D. L. Sheth. One of them is the first number of a very hopeful journal, *Alternatives*, edited by Rajni. In this last one there is a fine and lucid article—the very first one—by Fritz Schumacher.

As I read Fritz's article a whole host of memories crowded in my mind. The most vivid of them was how on two occasions I had Fritz invited (by the Planning Commission), how he visited Sokhodeora, spoke and stayed at the Varanasi Institute [36] and generally stimulated the Gandhians, the academicians, the scientists and others. On his last visit Mrs Gandhi made him stay for 45 minutes (D. P. Dhar, Deputy Chairman of the Planning Commission, had given him only 10 minutes and had expected the PM too to give him no more time). Mrs Gandhi at the end of the interview asked Fritz to give her in writing a few points on which she could ask her economic advisers to work. This Fritz did. But nothing came out of it. As Fritz writes in this article ('Alternatives in Technology'), 'government is never more than the executive of the prevailing system, implementing that system's philosophy'. This is much nearer the facts in the world today than Marx's definition, which was true at his time. (I might also recall here that when I founded the Gandhian Institute I invited Fritz to take up its Directorship for a few years. He was quite agreeable, indeed happy. But unfortunately at that very time his first wife died—of cancer, I believe—leaving behind a number of children. Fritz was still at the National Coal Board at that time. Anyway that tragedy upset all his plans. After a year or more

36. Gandhian Institute of Studies at Varanasi. It was started at JP's instance in the early 'sixties and he was its Honorary Director till 1972.

he married again and he had to start a new life. He could hardly think of coming to India nor could I think of pressing him to do so. I had met Fritz during our first visit—Prabha's and mine—to Great Britain and Europe. That was in 1958 perhaps. We were invited by the Socialist Union of which Rita Hinden was the moving spirit. Fritz also was in that Union. The Union is dead now, but the *Socialist Commentary* goes on, though Rita is also no more.)

Now, what would be the 'prevailing system' in India and its philosophy ? That is a very interesting question. Is there a system, first of all ? While 80 per cent of the population lives in the villages, 20 per cent of it is urban. Some of it is made up of industrial labour, some of the class IV employees and yet some more of the class III employees. Though there is much poverty and filth and slums in the urban areas, migration to the towns and cities goes on steadily. Only a small part of it finds employment, but the movement of population continues. Leaving out industrial labour and class III and IV employees, there are economically better-off people, a tiny part of them quite affluent in the Western style-of-living sense. Then there are students, school and university. There are officers of government and ministers (in the capital cities). If there is a system it is made up of these elements and the system's philosophy is that of the educated and economic elite. The elite from the rural areas are being constantly sucked into the urban areas.

What is the philosophy of this system ? To have more of what they have, to climb higher up and, on the radical fringes (socialist, communist, etc.), to see that more persons have what they have—i.e. spread the benefit. All politics, all education, all privileges are confined to this tiny layer of society at the top—not necessarily all capitalists, but all privileged—the public sector, leaving out agriculture, is perhaps the larger part of the industrial economy.

In India, this tiny layer of the elite, barring rare individuals, wants more modern technology, more industrialisation, more mechanization and chemicalisation of agriculture. That is the ethos of modernism in India. So, even if Fritz momentarily impressed Mrs Gandhi by his simple thesis, the system's philosophy buried it deep down.

The question of the Bihar movement and other similar movements getting involved with Opposition political parties has worried a number of friendly intellectuals and many well-wishers. I have been no less worried myself about it. As I look back I ask myself, did I make a mistake, and if so, what was it ? I have asked myself this question again and again during the movement also. What were, and are, the answers ? There is no doubt that if the movement had not got mixed up with Opposition parties, its character, its experimental utility, its educative value, its ability to enable the people to see their problems with their own eyes (not the eyes of the parties) and to think of their responsibility to do whatever lay in their power to solve their problems, to change themselves and change their material and social environment, and if they must offer peaceful resistance or non-cooperation in this process, to do so singly, in groups or in 'mass' (i.e., through a mass movement) would not have been compromised.

But the ideal never gets translated into practice without suffering deterioration. The first difficulty was, and will be again whenever the attempt is made anew, that it is just not possible to keep political parties from coming into an open mass movement. True, if the movement had been confined to the Sarvodaya workers alone and its principle was to keep away all political parties (including the ruling party), it would have been possible to keep them away. But, then, there would have been no *people's* movement.

Another aspect of this difficulty is that I did not *start* the movement. I had to take over what was on and give it direction, spread and depth. I am afraid, elsewhere and at other times other men wanting to build a people's movement will be faced with similar situations. Moreover, at its start, while the Bihar students' movement was truly a non-party affair and 80 to 90 per cent of the young men and women who participated in its programmes had no political party attachments, its leadership was surely made up of student and ex-student personnel who had strong party affiliations and who undoubtedly were guided by the party leaders outside. The parties involved were mainly four—Jana Sangh, Socialist Party, BLD and Congress (O). At several university centres the Jana Sangh was the strongest element, in some the BLD and the SP. The Congress (O) leadership in the Steering Committee was quite mature and influential, though numerically weak.

Now this was the situation when my association with the Bihar students' movement started. The political parties were there already. In fact, it will be admitted by all objective observers that my influence kept the party influences low, helped to evolve a consensus, and give the movement—at the start the students' movement and then the people's movement—a non-party political character.

There is yet another, and theoretically the most important, aspect of this problem of parties and a non-party people's movement. It is well known that both the Gujarat and Bihar movements started with certain demands or charges laid at the door of the State government : corruption (specially in government), unemployment, educational reform (or revolution) plus minor complaints about examinations, admissions, hostels, etc. Now, as I have said earlier in these Notes, it was up to the State government to have met the students in a friendly manner and discussed the demands seriously and done something about them. But when in either State the government chose the path of confrontation, a struggle *against* the government became inevitable. The situation immediately attracted the Opposition parties as honey attracts flies. What does one do in a situation like this ? The conclusion from this is that an attempt should be made to avoid a confrontation with the government, as Vinobaji wanted me to do. (His reasons, of course, were different, as I have explained earlier in these pages.) The question is can you do it ? No one, at least no one who has no party affiliation and therefore no motivation to exploit every situation for partisan ends, and who still is anxious to start a peaceful revolutionary movement, i.e., a movement to bring about basic changes in society and in social attitudes, can ever, in the conditions of our country, avoid a confrontation with the kind of government we have. But if the miracle happens and the government and the ruling party come forward to cooperate with the revolutionary movement, that would be something to celebrate, not to mourn. But I do not see the

Congress under Mrs Gandhi ever behaving thus. What about the Opposition parties ? Will they behave any better ? That is to be seen. I personally think they will, at least, in Bihar and hopefully in other States too, provided there were in those States popular movements of change.

This brings me to the last part of this question.

Is the involvement of the political parties in a Bihar-type people's movement an unmixed evil ? Its faults are obvious enough, as touched upon briefly in the foregoing and as articulated by every friendly and understanding critic. But in the first place, in an open movement involving the greater bulk of college students and the people, it is impossible to keep anyone out as I have shown above. After all, the parties that entered the movement in Bihar did not enter as parties, and their leaders, workers and sympathisers came in as individuals. These parties, of course, at their formal meetings outside the movement, passed resolutions and issued statements fully supporting the movement. But the question to ask is, is the participation of Opposition parties an unmixed evil ? My unhesitating answer is No. Its first result, too obvious to be argued, is that it lends strength to the movement. But the more important thing is that the parties undergo a sea-change in the process. True, this would not happen in a State where there is no strong non-party leadership in the movement. But in Bihar it has happened. All the parties involved are committed to the aims of total revolution and to the dynamics of change : struggle. This is no small gain. And I would invite the consideration of my intellectual friends to this great possibility. So far, we have seen students' and people's struggle in the form of confrontation with the government. In Bihar, after the next elections there is every possibility of witnessing a people's struggle in cooperation with the State government. I hope the baptism of fire through which the Opposition has passed and is passing in Bihar would have steeled their commitment to total revolution. I admit if God removes me from the scene before then, this will only remain a dream. But the experience will not have been lost and later someone else will come forward to pick up the thread.

September 7

I should add one thought to what I have written above. There is no possibility in sight and in the near future of India having any other type of democracy than she has today. Hopefully, if the Opposition wins the next parliamentary elections, the present Constitution and the electoral laws, rules, etc., might be improved. But the 'type' of democracy will not change much. Therefore, there seems to be no way for a people's movement (which term should mean to include the students and youth) to carry forward its programmes of revolution except in the context of a party (or a coalition of parties) government. The context may be malignant or benign as discussed above.

In respect of 'improvement' in the present type of democracy, I have mentioned constitutional and statutory amendments under an Opposition government. But there may be extra-constitutional and legal ways of doing it also. This can be possible only in the context of an on-going people's movement. These struggle committees or people's committees, or Navanirman samitis, *viplavi samitis* (whatever be the name given to the organs of people's struggles) may perform, as we were aiming to do, and we shall again try do so, the functions of (*a*) being sounding boards or consultation media at the time of candidate selection, and (*b*) acting as 'watch-dogs' and accountability-enforcers over their local representatives as well as over the whole working of the government. We hear so much these days of people's participation in this and that—Mrs Gandhi is the author of this deception. But it is all humbug. Once you gag the people's mouth and prevent them from expressing their sincere feelings and grievances, you are only adding insult to injury when you go about talking of people's co-operation and the people doing this and that. To-day the only thing the people are allowed to do is to sing the praises of Mrs Gandhi.

September 7

The Attorney-General makes it out that Parliament is supreme and can do what it wills with the Constitution : it can change any part of the Constitution any way it likes. This is a horrendous picture of our democracy. No wonder, Gandhiji called parliamentary democracy a dictatorship of the majority. What, genius had he to go to the very root of things ! If Mr De is right then the Constitution has to be drastically changed. The Supreme Court must clearly and categorically lay down what constitutes the 'basic structure' of our democracy, which Parliament cannot alter. Alternatively, the Supreme Court must clearly decide that the concept of a basic structure is a fiction and that there is no such thing at all. After all, the Constitution Bench of the Supreme Court might as well be abolished for all times.

Let us turn to politics. For MPs, no matter of which party, the words 'Parliament is supreme' must sound grand. They tickle their vanity, give them notions of supremacy and turn their heads. But politically what does the supremacy of Parliament mean ? It means something sordid, something revolting to a democrat. Parliament virtually means the Cabinet (it is as true of Great Britain as of India), the Cabinet means the leader, the PM. In a spineless party like the Congress the leader is a virtual dictator. In India the Cabinet means Mrs Gandhi. So when the sonorous words are pronounced 'Parliament is supreme', what is being declared is that Mrs Gandhi is supreme.

In another sort of party, like the Conservative Party or the Labour Party (of Great Britain), while the PM for the term may be much more than a mere 'first among equals,' as Wilson is, there is internal life and vigour and ,vitality within these parties and leaders have been replaced. Their performance counts far more than party management. The role of public opinion, shifts of opinion, the non-committed voters who often play decisive roles, the international situation, the prices of bread, butter and meat, the employment position—all these and several other factors play their role. Most important, the existence of two parties, capable of replacing each other depending upon the above-mentioned and other factors, also radically affects the 'dictator' position of the PM in the U.K. In India how different is everything ! So let not anyone be beguiled by the concept of the supremacy of Parliament. The concept just does not fit into the picture. Here there must be clearly laid down checks and balances. No organ of the State should be supreme. All this has to be very clearly worked out by competent persons sharing these views.

September 9

In that very valuable journal, *Alternatives*, edited by Rajni Kothari, the second article is by Jimoh Omo-Fadaka, entitled 'Development : The Third Way'. As I read the article I found the author propounding the same set of ideas as I have been putting forth since 1954. This has suggested to me that I better plan a short book in which I bring together the different theses I have propounded at different times and draw all the strings together to make a whole—not a crazy-quilt wholeness but a natural harmonious whole, the parts of which naturally fit with the other parts and all of them merge together into a harmonious form.

Let me set out the parts with which I have dealt with at one time or another.

I. *The Moral-Spiritual Framework*

(a) Man is both matter and spirit. His life must fulfil both his material and his spiritual needs.

(b) Material needs must be fulfilled—food, clothing, dwelling, etc. Food should be adequate, simple, nourishing and tasteful. But it should not be excessive. Clothes should be not only utilitarian but also pleasing to the eye and to the touch. It should be enough for all weathers. But there should be no excess, no craze for fashion, no wastefulness. Materials for clothing should be organic (as far as possible) and not inorganic and synthetic. Dwellings should be modest, fit for human living, (healthy ventilation, sunlight, etc). Large, ostentatious dwellings should be shunned. Luxury in living

:should be discouraged. Luxury being a relative term, it should relate to the social needs and general standards.

And so on with other material needs. This implies voluntary limitation on consumption, which is a moral concept. I do not have asceticism in mind. That is for spiritual seekers. For the average man, for all of us, except those who accept asceticism as a way of spiritual perfection or aim, a full material satisfaction is itself a spiritual life. Craving, excess, bad means to gather wealth, these are anti-spiritual.

Give the moral-spiritual reasons as well as economic, social, political, ecological, natural (renewability or otherwise, availability). Hazards of nuclear power for peace, etc.

The question of development for what, for whom, etc. The question of war and peace, of spiritual beauty and creativity.

Moral-spiritual constraints on material development.

II. The Natural-Environmental Framework

The question of village and town and city. Megalopolis and decaying countryside. Regrouping of villages—small villages to be merged, large villages to be re-distributed. Adivasī areas, hills and forests, and plains. Optimum size of villages in the plains. Optimum size of cities. Radial towns, i.e. small towns from where roads, power services, etc., radiate to the countryside. CD headquarters might be ideal centre for the development of such townships. Bank, store-houses, hospital.

This picture of geographical distribution of population—village, town, city—cannot be brought about by force. It presupposes and conforms to a type and process of socio-economic and political development which must be accepted democratically by the people and implemented democratically by the organs of the state and voluntary bodies.

III. Economic Framework

The aim of economic development should be Man. Work for every adult or head of family (wife and minor and unmarried children and old parents, unemployed brothers or cousins—Difficult question). Standard of living—minimum.

Perhaps in India we have enough of the large-scale, modern

technology, capital-intensive industries. We may deliberately call a halt to their growth, except what the needs of defence dictate. The costly, showy, non-utilitarian, so-called prestige-giving imitative enterprises such as the satellite development should be given up. Here the distinction that Fritz has drawn between scientific research and development and application of science to technology (such as moon-going and the rest) is accepted and stressed. I am not asking for scientific inferiority but only for applications of science which in the given conditions of India and the needs of the people are directly related to their well-being.

Industrial development should therefore take the line of medium industry, small industry, rural industry development. This would require upgrading of the technology in use in the rural and small industries. Vigorous problem-based research in the development of *appropriate* technology should be taken up and pushed ahead. The rural schools should have a rural technology section—practical and theoretical and related to local practices and needs.

Ownership pattern, individual (family) self-employed producer, community ownership (village), co-operative ownership, private profit-based small entrepreneur ownership who employs a moderate number of workers and pays adequately in terms of prevailing or legal minimum wages. Larger enterprises may be capitalist in pattern within certain restraints, but public corporation pattern should be more prevalent. The working of the public corporation, the issue of incentives for the directors and managers, democratic regulation, efficiency, waste, etc., should be deeply studied and guidelines laid down. In the present context can workers' ownership and managements succeed ? In large establishments workers' ownership cannot apply. There the concept of social ownership will have to be applied. But if the workers employed in the industry can manage it as *trustees*, trustee not only of their own interests but also of the consumer, the community and the society or nation at large, that from my point of view would be the best. The Yugoslav pattern minus the dictatorship could be quite an agreeable picture.

In the large sector, both public and private or public limited company ownership may be allowed to continue. The private sector should have enough incentives to produce, develop and grow.

Unnecessary restraints (controls, licences, etc.) should be removed, provided it meets certain standards of conduct laid down by law.

Workers' participation in management may be tried, but unless the trade unions train their representatives properly, the workers may not be effective in the realm of *management* proper. Their influence may be limited to workers' welfare—conditions of work, housing, schools, etc.

The large establishments particularly, but all productive units, including agriculture, must be keenly sensitive to ecological considerations, as well as considerations of beauty and cleanliness.

The neo-colonial exploitation of which Omo-Fadaka has written must be deeply studied in the case of India. I am not competent to do this, though I have a vague fear about it, which I have expressed.

IV.   The Political Framework
The fundamental freedoms, decentralisation, communitarian.

V.   Cultural Framework

VI.   Educational Framework
A rural school : agriculture, rural industry, economics, sociology (meaningful for the students of the area), science, language and literature, economics—cooperation and cooperatives—laws, rules, (constitution), gram sabha (decision-making and enforcement), *gram adalat*, accounts and book-keeping (agriculture, trade and rural industry), hygiene, sanitation (latrines, water supply), bacteria, biology (related to rural frame), horticulture, zoology, food and nutrition (sources available), gas plant, compost, urine-manure.

VII.   Social Framework

VIII.   The Dynamics of Change and Reconstruction

Today is Vinoba's birthday. He completes 80 years of his life today. May he live for a hundred years ! It appears from yesterday's and today's newspapers that his health has considerably improved. He has relief from cough as well as fever.

Received a letter from Mrityunjaya Babu. His postcard contains more information about the devastation of floods (in Bihar) than in a four-page letter from another friend. Only, he forgot to give any news of the Bihar Relief Committee. But he has little connection with that organisation. He has even said something about Ganga Babu, and also about the Gandhi Memorial Museum and Dr Razi Ahmed. Perhaps he has no information about the Mahila Charkha Samiti.

September 12

Congressmen, it seems, have gone all out to lionise Vinoba. One of them, Mr Khadilkar, seemed hardly to contain himself when he exulted : 'One single quality of Vinobaji was that he stood like a rock in the midst of a crisis in the Sarvodaya movement.' It is all so disgustingly cunning. Mrs Gandhi's plane dash to Vinoba, her overnight stay at the Ashram and now these fulsome words on the birthday celebrations in Delhi. Let us see what Mrs Gandhi does on the prohibition front : 'After all, it is a state subject you know. The Prime Minister can only write, advise and prod.' Poor Gokulbhai ! [37] I do sincerely hope that he takes full advantage of this turn of the tide in prohibition's fortune.

Though I decided many days ago to stop commenting on Mrs Gandhi's sayings, I have been wanting to make an exception and comment on her remarks (which she has repeated in different

37. Gokulbhai Bhatt, leader of the prohibition movement in Rajasthan. Earlier, he had undertaken a fast unto death in support of his demand for total prohibition. He gave up the fast on Vinoba's advice.

ways) on the students. Speaking of our attitude towards the students, again without naming me or any of my colleagues, she said 'for these people', students could do no wrong. They could burn buses, loot and do any kind of mischief, but for 'them' (meaning us) they were sacrosanct.

Inasmuch as students have played such a leading role in the Gujarat and Bihar movements, and they are likely to play such a role in future too, I feel that in all fairness to our students I should not let this slander on them or on me go unanswered.

It is true that students have on occasions set fire to buses, railway stations, pulled up railway tracks, beaten up their teachers, and done other similar things. No one with any sense of responsibility towards the student community and the youth generally of this country can condone such acts. Irresponsible political activists may have encouraged such action at times in the fond and mistaken hope that it is all a prelude to a revolution—a violent revolution. But apart from such elements, no one would condone student violence. Then what do you do about it ? Obviously, the most important thing is to try to *understand* the students. What makes them behave in this manner ? Some of the student 'leaders' might be criminally disposed and they might have their gangs of toughs and rowdies, who need not be students at all. But the phenomenon of student unrest is not caused by criminality. Its causes lie in the unsuitable and in some respects rotten educational system, in the frustrations of unemployment, and in the wrong-headed policies of socio-economic development. It is this root problem that Mrs Gandhi must grapple with, because she is Prime Minister and today a dictator for all practical purposes. But her 20 points even if they are implemented will only scratch the surface. And student unrest will burst forth with greater force one of these days.

But what could one like me and others who worked with me do ? We, of course, tried to understand student violence. I, at least, never condoned it or slurred it over. But positively what I tried to do was to turn the blind anger and fury of the youth to peaceful revolutionary channels. My influence over the Gujarat student movement was marginal. But in fairness to that pioneering movement it must be said that by and large the student leadership was against violence. Interestingly, the most virulent and fire-eating of the student leaders who openly spoke about violence is now within Mrs Gandhi's fold !

Coming to Bihar, whatever violence had taken place was before my association with the movement. After that the students behaved as disciplined soldiers, though most of them were not votaries of peaceful methods under *all* conditions. But barring that theoretical reservation they behaved peacefully, sometimes in the face of extreme provocation as on that memorable 4th of November, when we were tear-gassed and lathi-charged. I am not suggesting that there were no violent incidents during the movement. But the few that did take place were the result of extreme provocation by agents-provocateurs (mostly CPI men), or lack of leadership.

Therefore, it is wrong for Mrs Gandhi to say that for us students could do no wrong. We pointed out their wrongs whenever the occasion demanded and offered alternative courses of action.

But where was the Bihar movement going and how did I wish to bring about the revolutionary changes in education and in the socio-economic structure of society which alone could have satisfied the aspirations of the students ? The answer was coming forth steadily. But frightened by the revolutionary prospect, Mrs Gandhi has tried to bar the way. But the way cannot be barred permanently. I do not think it will ever be possible to bring about any revolutionary change in any sphere of the national life without the pressure and thrust of a 'movement'. Indeed, many changes will directly be wrought in the course of the movement itself; others may happen as the result of democratic legislation enacted in response to the movement. The changes directly brought about by people's action would need to be regularised later by legislation. The movement's pressure or thrust resulting in direct change or indirect (legislative) change may be of several kinds, such as persuasion (resulting from mass pressure), non-cooperation, civil resistance and civil disobedience. In the industrial field it may take the form of strike, direct take-over and management and 'running' of enterprises. (This would require a very mature working class and trade union unity.)

Here are the names of those whom I have written in the past 10 weeks :

1. Shivnath Prasad (brother-in-law)	1 letter Calcutta
2. T. Abraham (my secretary)	2 letters Patna
3. Gulab Yadav (my servant)	2 letters Patna
4. Jainarayan Sahaya (friend)	2 letters Patna
5. Jeevesh (Sister's grandson)	1 letter Patna
6. Gangasharan Sinha (friend)	1 letter Patna
7. Anil Prasad (nephew)	1 letter Bombay
8. Mrs Malti Singh (friend)	1 letter New Delhi
9. Rafiq Khan (friend)	1 letter Varanasi
10. Sugata Dasgupta (friend)	1 letter Varanasi
11. D. Buxi (nephew)	1 letter Patna
12. Sushila Sinha (friend)	1 letter Patna
13. Prabha Choudhary (friend)	1 letter Patna
14. Jagdish Singh (friend)	1 letter Ballia
15. Snehamayi Prasad (brother's wife)	1 letter Ballia
16. Vibha Singh (like my daughter)	1 letter Patna
17. Kusum Deshpande (like my daughter)	1 letter Paunar

Total : 20 letters

September 14

There is a UNI report in this morning's *Hindustan Times* of
Mr Brahmanand Reddy's speech at Madras at the end of which
are these lines : 'Answering a question, he said 30 per cent of
the arrested persons had been released by government.' I wish
he had been asked to give the total number of arrests and the
total number of those released, and also how many of those
arrested and released were political and how many smugglers,
etc.

This morning's *Tribune* publishes a PTI report of the same
speech giving it a 3-column heading saying '30 per cent of MISA
detenus already let off : Reddy'. Both reports agree on that,
though the *Tribune* plays it up while in the *Hindustan Times*
the report has a single-column heading saying 'Insurgency may
end soon : Reddy'. (Insurgency refers to the Naga-Mizo area.)

In the PTI report in the *Tribune*, Reddy is reported to have said (bold type story-lead) : 'With normalcy prevailing throughout the country, 30 per cent of those arrested under MISA since the promulgation of emergency have been released. .....' It is a significant admission by the Home Minister that normalcy prevailed throughout the country.

Chandigarh.
15-9-1975

To
The Home Secretary,
Government of India
New Delhi

Sir,
To date there has been no reply to my letter of 7-7-75 requesting for transfer to Bihar or to a place near the State. I am hereby repeating that request and hope this time it will elicit a favourable reply.

There is also another matter to which I wish to draw your attention.

Leaving out the current week starting from the 10th of this month, I have been in detention for ten weeks now. At the rate of 2 letters per week, according to the present rules, I have written 20 letters in all so far. Of these only one letter written to Kusum Deshpande seems to have reached its destination, as is obvious from her reply. There is no reply from any of the others, and I have positive information that most of the others have never reached the addressees concerned.

Some of the letters I have written were to relations and some to friends. A detenu is allowed to write both to relations and some friends. It was so in the times of the British too. Kusum Deshpande is not related to me in any way, though she is as dear to me as a daughter. (Of course, it is obvious why an exception has been made in her case).[38]

Now, Sir, the fact that 19 out of my 20 letters have been held

38. Kusum Deshpande is an inmate of Acharya Vinoba Bhave's *ashram* at Paunar.

back cannot just be a matter of censorship. I consider it to be a serious deprivation of my right as a detenu. In fact, it amounts to mental torture. I hope, therefore, this matter will be seriously considered and the wrong corrected.

Yours sincerely,
JAYAPRAKASH NARAYAN

September 18

Mr V. C. Shukla has given a certificate to the Press today—a headline : 'most newspapers now behaving well'. How wonderful ! These people seem to have lost all sense of proportion, all sense of values. They do not realise how ridiculous they appear. Mrs Gandhi's democracy, of course !

Moved tonight (8.30 p.m.) to one of the PGI's [39] guest houses. Fine lawn here for walking. Nurses will not attend. Dr Kalara will come morning and evening. Dr Khatri might drop in occasionally. Dr Chhuttani [40] and Dr Mehra may also come occasionally. This is one step forward towards normal health.

Dr. Kalara examined me at 9.30 p.m.—pulse 80, rest OK.

September 19

Being new to the place could not sleep well. Dr Kalara came at 7.45 a.m. Pulse rate was 80. Rest OK. Morning walk had to be given up due to Sun. From tomorrow morning walk 7.00 a.m.

September 20

This morning's papers report the proceedings of what is sugges-

39. Postgraduate Institute of Medical Education and Research at Chandigarh, where J P was detained.
40. Dr P. N. Chhuttani, Director of PGI.

tively called the First All-India Conference of 'Educators for Secularism, Socialism and Democracy'. Mrs Gandhi, of course, is the 'Chancellor' of this body of educators comprising such distinguished Vice-Chancellors and Professors and learned persons as Mrs Subhadra Joshi (Treasurer of the Educators), Dr K. L. Shrimali (President of the Educators), Professor Rasheeduddin Khan, and the rest.

So, now India and Indians have to be re-educated in secularism, socialism and democracy. The old educators—Gandhi, Nehru, Patel, Prasad, Azad, CR, and the rest of the fathers—have become out of date. And now Mrs Gandhi and the other educators named above and, of course, any number of toadies, *jee-huzurs*, commies, will teach us what these great principles are. The first lesson is, do not allow the Opposition to grow too strong (otherwise Mrs Gandhi, brave woman, may, be annihilated). The second lesson is, put the Opposition leaders in prison (or detention), suppress civil liberties, suppress freedom of the press. The third lesson is, having muted dissent and criticism and opposition, feed the people with lies and go on lying until all are brainwashed.

(I feel tired today—these comments will be continued tomorrow.)

Tarkunde came today. Points to note and comments to make tomorrow.

September 21

So, according to the frightened lady of New Delhi, we all—Mr Morarji Desai, Mr Asoka Mehta, Mr Atal Behari Vajpayee, Mr Chandrashekhar, Mr Ramdhan and a host of others—were planning to annihilate Mrs Gandhi, her family, the Chief Ministers and others supporting her. She does not make it clear how this was to be done and what exactly is meant by annihilation. I have called Mrs Gandhi 'the frightened lady of New Delhi'. Frightened, of course, she was—almost out of her wits—by the gathering public opinion against her. She was afraid she would lose the next election and therefore a strategy was planned out for her—by whom that is a mystery. But more of this later on. The point to note here is that it was not because of fright that

Mrs Gandhi told the Educators in Secularism, Socialism and Democracy about the nefarious plan of the Oppositionists to annihilate her and her family. She did it as part of her plan to mislead the people of India and the ill-informed people of the world. This lie was told deliberately to justify the suppression of democracy. As time passes, I think she would come out with more daring lies. After all, there is none to contradict her, and if there is, there is no means of publishing the rejoinder except perhaps through surreptitiously printed and circulated leaflets, which cannot go far.

Tarkunde told me yesterday that Mrs Gandhi's one-sided propaganda was already having its effect. He found 'intellectuals' in Bombay already shaking their heads and saying, 'after all, look, there is more discipline now, and surely, the Oppositionists had gone too far'. So, the betrayal of the intellectuals has started. The rats have begun to leave the sinking ship !

To go back to Mrs Gandhi's performance at the 'Educators' conference. I shall only put down certain excerpts from the report of her speech in the *Hindustan Times* (September 20).

My guess, expressed earlier has all along been that Mrs Gandhi's action was not a sudden reaction to the decision taken on 25th June to press for her stepping down from the Prime Ministership until the Supreme Court had decided her appeal, and to that end to recruit Satyagrahis to march to her residence (or as near it as they were allowed) and thus offer civil disobedience. The policy as I had apprehended, had been thought out and planned in some detail much earlier. The 25th June resolution might have had something to do with the timing of the blow that came down on the head of Indian democracy in one fell swoop. But there is no doubt that it had been planned that Mrs Gandhi and those who supported her in the Congress and the CPI should never, never be dislodged from power, no matter what the people or the voters felt and wanted. The aim having been set, the ways and means were carefully worked out much in advance. The Bihar movement and the Delhi Satyagraha planned for a week and announced on the 25th at the public meeting were only convenient excuses. This is what she is reported to have said :

'We have not drifted in this direction', she said, adding that

72

"the path had been chosen after deep thought and deliberation and after weighing every possible alternative.' (*Hindustan Times*, September 20).

The question is where was this planned. Not in the Congress Working Committee, otherwise it would have been known. Was it ever approved by the CWC? Does not seem to be so. Was it planned in the Political Affairs Committee of the Cabinet or in the so-called 'Inner Cabinet' (the identity of whose members no one knows about)? The answer seems to be No. Did the Home Minister have any idea of the magnitude, sweep and intention of the plan? The answer, again, seems to be No. Obviously, it was planned in a secret cell of the PM's confidants, comprising almost certainly pro-Soviet members, one or more of whom must be in close touch and regular communication with some India cell in Soviet embassy. I am sure the secret will be out one day, but this is as far as my guess goes.

Here is another excerpt :

'Democracy', she said, 'was ultimately the voice of the people. We have not gagged the people. Very few people were in detention and even today some Opposition members were organising satyagraha and things like that.'
Mrs Gandhi said she was not against the Opposition, criticism or satyagraha. But she was opposed to a small minority trying to gag a vast majority.

She did not clarify how a small minority was trying to *gag* a vast majority. Where was this done and how? A small minority with arms may be able to do so. A small minority in power might be able to do so. But how can a peaceful movement try to do so? And what does gagging mean? The Congress show at Patna on 16 November 1974 was a miserable failure in spite of the free ride on buses, trains, trucks, steamers; in spite of free food supplied on the way and some new clothing distributed too. The Congress was in power and the entire administration tried to make it a grand success. And there was Mrs Gandhi's wonder boy, Mr Borooah on the scene to offer the benefits of his powerful brain and to master-mind the whole operation. Was a single instance of anyone 'gagging' a single individual reported or any-one preventing anyone, physically, from going to Patna ? And the public meeting on 18th November ? Was that not an instance of a small minority gagging the vast majority ?

Mrs Gandhi is reported to have referred to satyagrahas even now being organised by the Opposition. This is the first time I have read of satyagrahas in the midst of the totalitarian deluge. I have seen nothing about it in the papers. However, if Mrs Gandhi is not lying again, I am glad this is happening. It means the fire is still there and its flames do appear here and there, now and then. This is what used to happen in the case of Gandhiji's satyagraha movements.

Mrs Gandhi says, 'We have not gagged the people.' Good. The proof of the pudding will be in the eating. Democracy, she says, is ultimately the voice of the people !

Well, she did not listen to the voice of the people in Bihar, even though it was so unmistakable in its expression. She said that the issue will be settled at the next elections. I accepted her challenge.

The reason for the eating of the pudding, for its proof, is coming. According to the philosophy of Mrs Gandhi, the voice of the people should be and can be expressed only at elections. At no other time, apparently, has the voice of the people any validity or even the right to be expressed. The only exception is when the 'people' voluntarily come crowding before her residence begging her not to resign, not to leave them orphans. At that time the people's voice has great validity and must be listened to and obeyed ! Oh, this hypocrisy, this cant !

The elections to the Lok Sabha are due early next year. Let us see if the voice of the people is going to be gagged for their benefit or is allowed to be expressed through voting ballots.

There is a picture on the front page of the *Tribune* (September 20) of the inaugural session of the First Conference of the Educators, etc. My friend, Dr K. L. Shrimali is shown sitting next to Mrs Gandhi. There is such a look of smug satisfaction, of one who has definitely 'arrived', on Shrimali's face. Somehow, as I looked on that face, I was reminded of the anguished and bitter look on his face when he was dropped by Nehru from his Cabinet (he was Minister of State for Education) as part of the Kamaraj

74

plan because according to Shrimali, he was not prepared to allot the sums he was wanted to for Dhirendra Brahmachari's Yoga Ashram—Mrs Gandhi being personally interested at that time in Dhirendra Brahmachari and his Ashram. And she was angered by Shrimali's attitude and saw to it that he was dropped by her father in the ministerial reshuffle. According to Shrimali, Dr K. G. Saiyidain [41] himself was sent by Nehru to persuade Shrimali, but the latter stuck to his guns on the ground that the Yoga Ashram did not deserve support because money given to it before had not been properly accounted for. He had also raised some academic questions. Well, the upshot was the exit of the Education Minister. How bitter he was then and how critical! And now this look of beatitude on the Vice-Chancellor's face! How people change!

September 24

Finished Bertrand Russell's third volume of autobiography. The picture of the man that emerges from this volume is highly attractive, admirable and noble. Someone has described him as 'an ornament of civilisation'. It is a beautiful description. To me Bertrand Russell is an ornament of humanity. There is hope for this race of creatures because of the Bertrand Russells that have emerged from its womb from time to time—maybe once in a few centuries.

The Postscript at the end of this volume is very moving. The closing words sum up the mature Russell :

'I have lived in the pursuit of a vision, both personal and social. Personal : to care for what is noble, for what is beautiful, for what is gentle; to allow moments of insight to give wisdom at more mundane times. Social : to see in imagination the Society that is to be created, where individuals grow freely, and where hate and greed and envy die because there is noth-

41. The late Dr K. G. Saiyidain was Educational Adviser to the Government of India and a member of the Education Commission 1964-66.

ing to nourish them. These things I believe, and the world, for all its horrors, has left me unshaken.'

What a noble vision, faith in the future !

September 25

This was a day of great joy. It was a day of a most pleasant surprise. Sugata [42] suddenly appeared in the doorway followed by the Deputy Commissioner. I embraced him and asked 'how come'? It happened that he met P. N. Dhar at a UGC [43] meeting at Delhi. In the course of his conversation he told him he was very anxious to see me. Dhar said, 'Why not ? Go and see him.' Sugata asked if the meeting will be restricted to so many minutes. Dhar said, no, he was free to take his time. It was kind of Dhar. I told Sugata to tell him from me that I was grateful, but alas, that Dhar to my mind had fallen in bad company ! Sugata came a second time in the evening. The D.C. was present all through.

September 26

Have completed three months of detention today. Now the days seem to be passing fairly quickly. Still lack of company makes time hang heavily, but it appears that the fall into the pit of totalitarianism has been halted, whether temporarily or permanently it is too early to judge. Sugata was saying yesterday that there was general expectation in the circles he moved in that parliamentary elections would be held next year. If that happens, the return to democracy will be a certainty, though the Emergency may not be revoked and the press may not be completely freed. But jail delivery will be certain and there will be greater freedom of speech and association.

42. Mr Sugata Dasgupta, Director of the Gandhian Institute of Studies, Varanasi set up by J P.
43. University Grants Commission.

September 28

Yesterday (September 27, Saturday) was a bad day for me. In the morning as I sat on the water closet there was terrible pain in the stomach. At first I thought it would pass off. But it continued and became more severe. I began to perspire copiously, felt faint and very weak. Had difficulty in getting up, washing and returning to my bed. I asked for Dr Kalara to be called and also Dr Chhuttani to be informed. The pain continued for hours. The doctors gave medicines. Was in bed the whole day. Took only liquids and at night a little rice with curds. The diagnosis is some infection. Whatever it be this was the first experience of its kind in my life. Because of the profuse perspiration and pain and weakness I thought at first I had a heart attack—but the pain was in the lower abdomen. Heart, BP, etc., were normal. The ECG was taken and nothing new was found.

Today I feel much better. Just had a 20 minute walk in the lawn—6.30 p.m.

September 29

The *Tribune* has a 3-column headlined speech of Mr Jagjivan Ram, asserting with great force, 'PM's Leadership Vital For Executing 20-Point Plan'. I wonder why this loud declaration of loyalty. Is there a hidden reason behind it, or is it just a periodical reaffirmation of loyalty ? It is incredible that such sycophancy should be so loudly exhibited even by a man like Jagjivan Babu. What a degeneration !

It is a pity that no one asked Mr Ram why the dear PM's leadership failed in the case of the 10 points ? Perhaps it was the perfidy of the Opposition that was to blame !

This morning's *Tribune* also announces that total prohibition is likely. How wonderful ! In spite of the political trickery involved, it would be a most welcome consummation. The political trickery, of course, is to win over Vinoba and the Sarvodaya movement more securely and show up and expose Jayaprakash and his friends and their ill-conceived and mischievous opposition to such a devout Gandhian as Mrs Gandhi. This would also help in the coming elections. Well, I do not mind it at all. Let Mrs Gandhi get the kudos and let Jayaprakash be damned. So far as I am concerned the fight for democracy and the fight against corruption, misrule, etc., will continue. Total revolution still remains my goal.

September 30

President Sadat of Egypt seems to tower over all the leaders, not only of West but of entire Asia. Chairman Mao Tse-tung is a class by himself and he, no doubt, is a colossus. But leaving him out, there is no one today in Afro-Asia who can compare with Sadat. I have in mind his Cairo speech at the fifth anniversary of President Nasser's death. The boldness and frankness with which he has spoken of Russia being 'on my back', when the US sent new deadly weapons and American experts to Israel. That is how he had to accept the cease-fire on 22 October 1973. 'The turning point in his relations with the Soviet Union had come in 1972 when former President Richard Nixon visited Moscow.' A joint statement on the visit had called for a military relaxation in West Asia "at a time when I was not fully armed, 10 steps behind the Israelis and with my land occupied". (*Tribune*, September 30) 'The President said the statement had been the straw that broke the camel's back.' The whole speech is remarkable and I am keeping a clipping.

Is there anyone in the ruling circles in our country who can speak with such forthrightness and boldness ? This is patriotism of the highest order. God knows how deep the Russians have penetrated into our decision-making and vital organs of government and polity.

October 1

A *Hindustan Times* headline says 'Varsity Can't be Sanctuary from Law'—PM. Quite right. But Ministership too cannot be sanctuary from law and Prime Ministership less than any other. This was the whole point of the 'movement'. Those elected to positions of power cannot be outside the scope of the law. Therefore, the demand was that there should be created an institutional body—like the Swedish Ombudsman—to keep those in power accountable to law and to the people. In this connection the Santhanam report and other recommendations of students of the problem (like A. G. Noorani) were suggested as a basis for discussion and decision by consensus. But the worthy PM considered herself and her colleagues in the States and at the Centre to be unaccountable to anybody until the next general elections decided the issue of power. This not only encouraged licence by those in office, but also ensured, through the use of money power and electoral corruption (which is easier for those in power to indulge in than for those in opposition), that those in power would come back to power again, thus perpetuating misrule, corruption and the rule of a clique or caucus.

Even to date, though the PM has taken certain steps to meet half way the issues raised by the movement, she has done nothing to set up an Ombudsman (I am using this term as a sort of shorthand) or any other body or procedure by which the people could have a greater say in the choice of candidates and some control over the elected representatives and make them continuously accountable.

Mrs Gandhi is lecturing a great deal these days on 'discipline' and pats herself on the back quite frequently for the new climate of discipline in the country due to the Emergency proclamation. But she has yet to realise—I fear this she will never be able to do—that the climate of indiscipline in the country was created by the arrogance, inefficiency, corruption and in-fighting of and within the ruling party and clique. Mrs Gandhi herself gave a fine example of discipline when she formally nominated Mr Sanjiv Reddy for Presidentship but worked for Mr V. V. Giri who, (as a Congressman) breaking party discipline was fighting against the official Congress candidate. This glaring piece of political indiscipline and disloyalty is excused on the ground of *politics being politics*, meaning that you cannot look closely into the ethics of political conduct. Mrs Gandhi, of course, only compounded her political immortality by invoking a convenient 'conscience'.

If India and the Indian people have to be put through totalitarian rigours in order to be taught the virtue of discipline, that virtue would be found at the first test to have been a mere veneer. Discipline is a quality of individual and group behaviour which has to be inculcated and nurtured in an atmosphere of freedom, i.e., in a condition in which there is a choice of action. In this process, especially in a society like ours in which political power and politics occupy such a dominant position (which is but a fact regrettable) the inculcation of discipline depends, more than on anything else, on the behaviour of those in power and government. Any objective assessment of the morality of the Indian political parties in 1974-75 would have shown the ruling Congress to be easily the most corrupt and politically immoral of all. There were honest people in the Congress, no doubt, and there still are, but they had to take the back row in a situation in which intrigue, bribery, cupidity, sycophancy and other similar virtues hold such sway. Mrs Gandhi herself did not present such a clean picture of herself. Beginning with the Presidential election, there were a number of scandals which though they exercised the public mind so much remained a closed book owing to her persistent refusal to have any of them enquired into. The Nagarvala and Rs 60 lakh episode is still an unexplained mystery and the foreign trade licence scandal never became subject to public or judicial enquiry. Even parliamentary debate and probe were obstructed and played down. The Mishra murder, undoubtedly related to the licence scandal, still remains inadequately probed and exposed. The many issues connected with Maruti never became a subject of enquiry. The PM satisfied her conscience and tried to allay public doubts by issuing chits to her son. It is possible that there was really nothing shady in the Maruti business, but this had to be established by an impartial enquiry, which has been persistently refused. Within the political system,

80

the collection of huge election funds, unrestrained use of money power in elections, buying up of Opposition MPs and MLAs with money or jobs, and several other immoral deeds of the kind were perpetrated with impunity. The State Congress governments had earned a similar reputation for corruption and nepotism. Bihar was the most ill-reputed. In this atmosphere of 'modern politics' as some apologists of the regime called it, discipline as defined today by Mrs Gandhi (*Hindustan Times*) as 'self-control' and 'self-regulation' must remain a pious wish.

Mrs Gandhi is advising everyone to do some 'rethinking' during this black night of Indian democracy. I am sure everyone must be doing this even without Mrs Gandhi's prompting. But it does not appear that she herself is doing any re-thinking, or if she is, it is not in the direction of restoring health to the body-politic but of perpetuating her power, the sole objective of all her actions hitherto. Take this Emergency itself. From all accounts it seems to be an undoubted fact that there is calm and quiet in the whole country. This is sometimes proclaimed with pride by herself and her colleagues—pride over the success in putting down all unrest and opposition. There can be no justification then for prolonging the Emergency, except to enable Mrs Gandhi to stick to unchallenging power. October has come, but Mrs Gandhi is still vague and wary about the coming parliamentary elections. Perhaps she will not hold the elections until she has satisfied herself that her Operation Brainwashing has succeeded enough and the Opposition has been satisfactorily emasculated and rendered impotent. In that case, I am afraid, she will have to wait long and the night that has descended upon the country may never lift, because I cannot imagine how she can ever succeed in achieving these ends. Prolongation of the Emergency and the accompanying repression and denial of democratic rights are likely to have just the opposite result, no matter how far the betrayal of the intelligentsia may go. I have unshakable faith in the people and the country's youth and students. I have written about this before, so I shall not speak any further about it.

I am sorry to see that Jagjivan Babu seems to have so completely crumbled up. He too has taken up the refrain, along with Mrs Gandhi and Borooah, about 'saving democracy'. It is like the Americans trying to "save" the South Vietnamese by destroying them. Oh, there will be a lot of 'intellectuals' who will rush forward to show how a growing sapling has to be fenced in to be saved, how a child is to be protected from itself so that it may grow, etc., etc. But after all the arguments have been exhausted it is still doubtful if the Emergency, the sweeping arrests, the suppression of the press, if these and many other things done since 26 June last, have saved Indian democracy. I am strongly persuaded that these measures have dealt a grievous body blow to our democracy from which it will take long to recover. And if Mrs Gandhi and her caucus perpetuate themselves in power by one democratic hoax or another, it may never recover until a revolution, I still hope a peaceful one, sweeps the usurpers off the stage and restores freedom and democracy. A violent revolution, or an attempt at it, can either strengthen the usurpers' power or substitute them with another caucus of usurpers. This unfortunate country would then be set on the same path of misery, autocracy and degradation as so many other countries of Afro-Asia. Heaven save India from this fate!

October 2

'Art does not depend on the tomb, but on eternity. All sacred art is opposed to death, because it is not an adornment of the civilization it represents, but the expression of its highest values.'
—Andre Malraux, *Anti-Memoirs*, p. 32.

(Translated from Hindi) **October 2**

Bapu, I offer my salutations at your feet. Victory be to Mahatma Gandhi! Long live Mahatma Gandhi!

Today is the 106th birthday of Bapu. Nearly twenty-eight years have passed since his departure. During this period, everybody swore by his name, but very little of his work was done. For some years now the intellectuals of the country have been feeling that by deviating from Bapu's path, India committed a

82

great blunder. But these very intellectuals or others similar to them in Jawaharlal's time looked upon Gandhiji as a conservative and praised the "modern" outlook of Nehru. Mrs Gandhi, who has mastered the art of deception, has often claimed that she is only following the path of Gandhiji. Perhaps she will express similar sentiments even today on the occasion of his birthday celebrations. But all this is a fraud.

Vinobaji did something miraculous for some years. It appeared as though a new Gandhian process of social change and reconstruction had emerged. But after his stormy Bhoodan experiment, not even a mild breeze blew, not to speak of a mighty "storm" of Gramdan, Gram-Swarajya or any other constructive experiment. Later, he withdrew into his inner self, and started the experiment of 'action', in the form of 'inaction'. To date this does not seem to have borne fruit. But what is a period of 10 or 20 years in history? Meanwhile, the country is heading for a downfall, not only moral but also the economic, social and cultural degradation of at least 40 per cent of the Indian people who live below the poverty line. One is reminded here of a statement of Bapu who, while defining democracy, had said that it did not only mean a government established by the people's vote; it also meant that the people had the power to oust their rulers when found unworthy to rule. Democracy has almost ceased to exist in India today. The pyramid of the political structure still stands on its apex. The same is true of the educational and almost all other spheres of public activity. It is a tragic story that beggars description.

October 3

Kamaraj died yesterday in Madras of a massive heart attack. A great, even heroic figure of Indian politics is no more. His life's work was not complete yet. The last time he met me in Delhi, he said something like this: 'What you are doing is the only hope for the country.' But when I toured Tamil Nadu later, he was not pleased with my speeches. I could not condemn the DMK and call for a struggle against the Tamil Nadu government.

The reason was that Mr Karunanidhi, unlike the Congress Chief Ministers, offered to meet the Opposition and discuss with them their criticism of the DMK government. He said he was prepared even for an impartial enquiry into their faults, charges of corruption or of any other kind. In fact, he mentioned that in one case he had actually appointed a High Court judge as a commission of enquiry. He also pointed to the Public Men's Conduct Enquiry Act he had already had enacted and expressed his preparedness to discuss either with me or Opposition leaders any faults that the Act might be found to possess, such as the deterrent punishment provided in it for anyone whom the due process of law, as laid down in the Act, found to have wilfully made false charges. Under these conditions, a responsible Opposition was expected to take the DMK leader at his word and make a serious attempt to take the obvious steps. In fact, in one of my speeches in Tamil Nadu I urged Kamaraj to take up this therapeutic line and clean up the murky political climate in the State.

I am not suggesting that whatever Karunanidhi, Raja Ram,[44] Sezhiyan [45] told me in Madras or Delhi had to be taken at face value, or that I took it in that way. But in the absence of any response from Kamaraj and the Opposition it did not seem fair, at least for me, to attack the DMK government and give a call for a people's movement against it. A people's movement could still be developed (because, as I have endeavoured to show, it need not in every case be against the government; the latter may honestly cooperate with the movement because its objectives are far wider : a total revolution) but naturally Opposition leaders in Tamil Nadu, including Kamaraj, were not interested in any movement unless at least its immediate political aim coincided with the Opposition's aim.

For Kamaraj the situation was made more difficult—as compared for instance, with that of MGR [46] because (as he had told me at the Delhi meeting) he did not want to weaken the DMK

44. Raja Ram, DMK leader.
45. Era Sezhiyan, DMK member of the Lok Sabha.
46. M. G. Ramachandran, leader of the ADMK (Anna Dravida Munnetra Kazhagam).

as otherwise the ADMK would be correspondingly strengthened. For Kamaraj, the ADMK was even worse than the DMK. Yet, owing to the national policy of the Congress (O), he did not want to draw the Congress (I) nearer to him. Thus, unlike other States in India, the position of Kamaraj as a Congress (O) leader was a very uncomfortable and delicate one. As he told me he did not trust Mrs Gandhi in the least and *vice versa*. But in the quadrangular politics of Tamil Nadu, being openly opposed both to the DMK and the ADMK, he had little elbow room to manoeuvre. He knew that an unscrupulous politician like Mrs Gandhi would have no qualms about joining hands with the ADMK and he dreaded that eventuality. So, tentatively his position was to 'go it alone' at the next election. He realised that that would be disastrous for his party. However he preferred to wait and see. But for his party's national policy, reinforced by the Bihar movement and its national repercussions, he would have eventually thrown in his lot with Mrs Gandhi. His position and the options open to him further complicated and narrowed down after the proclamation of the Emergency and the consequent events.

However, death has settled that issue for him. His followers, I am afraid, will break up and disintegrate. Mrs Gandhi by deciding to attend his funeral has already dealt a severe blow to the Tamil Nadu Congress (O). Morarjibhai is in detention, the Congress (O) President, Ashok Mehta is also in detention. I doubt if C. B. Gupta's health will permit him to undertake the journey or whether he would have gone if his health were better. So, Mrs Gandhi will make the best of the situation. Somehow, I am reminded here that Mr Nehru did not think it necessary, either as protocol or as a moral obligation towards an old comrade-in-arms, to attend the funeral of Rajen Babu, though President Radhakrishnan had the humility of office and personal regard and affection enough to attend the funeral at Bansghat, Patna. For the Nehrus it seems politics decide everything !

October 4

Kamaraj's funeral seems to have been a truly human event. Sincere, moving, touching.

A 4-column headline in the *Tribune* proclaims : 'Complete Peace in India, says PM'. How wonderful ! As if before the Emergency there was countrywide absence of peace. Yet that is the refrain of Mrs Gandhi's song nearly everyday.

Asked about the parliamentary elections due next February-March, Mrs Gandhi has said, 'I cannot say yet. It is a long time to go. We don't usually consider it so far ahead of time.' It is a long time to go indeed ! October, November, December, January. Just four months left. Opposition leaders in jail. Press and platform shackled. An atmosphere of terror pervading the land. Is it expected that jail delivery and freedom of speech and association restored just on the eve of elections, say, in December end or January beginning, would give a fair chance to the Opposition to put its house in order, forge some kind of electoral unity —like the Gujarat Janata morcha (if not merging of the principal Opposition parties)—raise funds, etc., etc., in such a short time ? It is possible that Mrs Gandhi's strategy is exactly to do that.

October 5

Raja, Lal Babu and Abraham [47] came. Had a good interview, but all three had so much to tell me, I could not do justice to the interview. So many things I had to tell them, so many questions to ask, but most of them remained in my mind. There was not enough time. For the future I shall suggest that they do not all come together. This applies to others too.

Was very glad to learn that Sudha [48] and Uma [49] have been

47. T. Abraham, J P's Secretary.
48. Daughter of J P's younger sister.
49. Sudha's husband.

released and also Janaki [50] and Prashant.[51] They brought a letter from Janaki which I may get today or tomorrow after the censor has gone through it.

Raja met Nayantara [52] at Delhi. Might meet her again on way back. Babuni is in Patna.

No one has got my letter. Only two letters sent to Patna in July to Gulab [53] and Jeevesh [54] have been delivered. This government does seem mightily afraid even of inoffensive personal letters ! Or is it just pettiness ?

October 6

Learnt today that Sugata has reported in full to the Professor (Dhar) on his talks with me. This is good. Something seems to be moving at last. I wonder if Sugata will come back. Perhaps my letter to Sheikh Saheb has been sent to him or he has been told about it. Some move from that end is also possible.

(Translated from Hindi) **October 7**

TOTAL REVOLUTION

I have spoken and written a great deal on Total Revolution. Perhaps I have spoken, and not written, on this subject. Parts of my speeches have been compiled and even published in Hindi and English. Here I would try to formulate my thoughts more systematically.

I have been saying that total revolution is a combination of seven revolutions—social, economic, political, cultural, ideological or intellectual, educational and spiritual. This number may be

50. Miss Janaki Pande, Sarvodaya youth worker.
51. Kumar Prashant, a Sarvodaya youth activist in Bihar.
52. Nayantara Sehgal, Jawaharlal Nehru's niece and well-known writer.
53. Personal servant of J P.
54. Grandson of J P's elder sister.

increased or decreased. For instance, the cultural revolution may include educational and ideological revolutions. And if culture is used in an anthropological sense, it can embrace all other revolutions. But what we understand by culture in the context of a primitive society is not generally the same as in the context of a civilised society. Likewise, social revolution in the Marxian context covers economic and political revolutions and even more than that. This is how we can reduce the number to less than seven. And we can add to this number by breaking up each of the seven revolutions into different categories. Economic revolution may be split up into industrial, agricultural, technological revolutions, etc. Similarly, intellectual revolution may be split up into two—scientific and philosophical. Even spiritual revolution can be viewed as made up of the moral and spiritual, or it can be looked upon as part of the cultural. And so on. The important thing is that the technical words that we use must be clearly defined. As we know, the main difficulty in understanding the *Gita* is semantic. The *Gita* has used certain words giving them its own meaning; for instance, the word 'Yajna'.

Therefore what we understand by the seven revolutions must be spelt out clearly.

Economic Revolution

It means revolution in the economic structure of society and its economic institutions, as also their new, revolutionary forms. Economic revolution implies both change and new creation.

Everything is subject to change in this world. It is constantly changing and becoming new. What then does revolution or revolutionary change imply ? One implication is that the process of revolution or revolutionary change is very rapid, very far-reaching and radical too, and sometimes it leads to qualitative change in the object of change. For example, water when heated becomes steam.

October 10

Sugata came again. (October 8) This time the initiative came from Professor Dhar who telephoned him at Varanasi and asked him to go to Delhi to meet him. Sugata accordingly went to Delhi and Dhar had a long talk with him and asked him to go to Chandigarh and talk things over with me. Dhar was keen that the whole business should be kept strictly confidential and secret. At our talks the DC, though he came with Sugata, was not present. He sat in an adjoining room. We had nearly two hours' talk. There were no specific questions, answers to which Dhar wanted from me. The main issue or problem that Dhar wanted to be discussed with me was what I would do if I were released. I told Sugata that obviously Dhar could not expect me, after all that had happened, to support or cooperate with Mrs Gandhi. For the rest, the course of my future action would depend on the situation outside. Also, I would naturally want to consult my Sarvodaya colleagues and Opposition leaders. If they are not released along with me, there could be no consultation with them. And I would not want to consult them in detention. In any case, I was quite clear in my mind that if parliamentary elections are announced to be held at the scheduled time, I would advocate stoppage of the confrontation with government and call for an all-out effort to win the elections. But for that the Emergency should be revoked, democratic freedoms, including freedom of the press, should be restored and the leaders and workers in jail or detention must be released in good time. But if these things do not happen, if elections, under the pretext of emergency, are postponed and the democratic rights and liberties of the people, the press, the parties are not restored, then it is obvious that the confrontation must continue. In that case, if I am released, I shall try to reorganise the revolutionary forces and refashion, if necessary, the concrete programmes of action.

Incidentally, Dhar gave to Sugata my letter to Sheikh Saheb to be returned to me because she (i.e. Mrs Gandhi) did not want the Sheikh to play any role of negotiator or conciliator. I returned the letter to Sugata and asked him to keep it with him and use it as he thought fit. I also gave Sugata a copy of my first letter to the PM (July 21). Sugata also told me a lot of tit-bits and news that the papers have not published.

As Sugata was to stay another day, he came again on the 9th and again we had a long talk. He wanted to get my views restated so that he would not make any mistake while reporting to Dhar.

By the way, Dhar had made it clear to Sugata that he was taking the initiative at the specific instance of the PM.

Now I do not know what all this means and what the outcome will be.

Healthwise, 8th was again a bad day for me. Mostly intestinal trouble. Stomach felt like bursting from within, even though it was soft to the touch from the outside. No appetite. Constipation —not even gas passing. Had 99.2° temperature in the evening. There seems to be some infection in the intestine and inflammation. Dr. Chhuttani has prescribed Stemetil and Nevaquin tablets. Unienzyme has been resumed. I am also taking activated charcoal tablets. Feel much better today (October 10) though weak and exhausted.

October 11

I have completed 73 years of my life today. What a wonder! It is God's grace that in spite of long-term chronic diseases I have lived so long. May God grant me the wisdom and the will to devote whatever time is left for me to the service of the country and the people. That is the only way I have known to serve God. May He cleanse my heart and mind of everything impure.

Though I had not told anyone here (except one of the police officers in the course of a conversation) I was pleasantly surprised to see Sardar Mohinder Singh, Executive Magistrate and Superintendent of the jail, walk into my room with a large bouquet of flowers as birthday greetings. It is so kind of him.

"The State swells up, the people shrink."—pre-revolutionary historian Klychevesky referring to the Tsarist state, quoted by Bertram Wolfe in *Khrushchev and Stalin's Ghost*, p. 149.

No one came to interview in the past week. Mrs Gandhi cannot get over the fact that the Western press and Western leaders evince so much concern over the present eclipse of Indian democracy. In every interview with news agencies or journals Mrs Gandhi harps on the theme that while the Western press and leaders do not show any concern over such non-democratic countries like Pakistan, China, etc., they seem to be so exercised over the future of democracy in India. The simple point that while countries like China and Pakistan never were democracies (as we understand the term), India has been since its independence up to 26th June last a functioning democracy of which we were so proud and which we never let an opportunity go to stress in our international dealings and propaganda. When such a country which has been a democracy until a few months ago suddenly becomes authoritarian, it does draw the anxious attention of the democratic West and cause concern, even perhaps consternation. And when the West also feels that the grounds put forward by Mrs Gandhi for proclaiming the Emergency, amending the electoral law, amending the Constitution, arresting and detaining top political leaders for months together without trial—the grounds put forward for these undemocratic and totalitarian measures are the flimsiest imaginable, the concern of the Western press and leaders becomes even deeper. The lies and distortions and misrepresentations in which Mrs Gandhi has been indulging since 26th June cannot fool the West because it knows the real state of affairs. Nobody except the enemies of democracy can be taken in by Mrs Gandhi's hysterical propaganda.

Mrs Gandhi knows all this very well and yet she must protest against anyone outside India criticising her action. She has called the BBC anti-India today. Apparently, Mrs Gandhi cannot distinguish herself from India. For her India *is* Mrs Gandhi. *Ergo* anyone who is anti-Mrs Gandhi is anti-India !

Mrs Gandhi has been saying in and out of season, 'I did not even lose my temper.' Whether she lost her temper or not, she clearly lost her *nerve*.

Klychevesky's saying, quoted above, applies fully to Mrs Gandhi's rule : The State swells up, the people shrink. The only amendment I should like to make is to substitute 'Mrs Gandhi' for 'State'. From the way she has been talking these past months, it is clear that her head has swollen up. She apparently thinks that she has done something very big by proclaiming Emergency, suppressing the people's freedoms and the freedom of the press. She should rather be ashamed of herself that she has taken these retrograde and reactionary steps only to be able to cling to power.

(Translated from Hindi) **October 15**

Yesterday I finished the commentary on the *Gita* by Satyavratji. I like this commentary, which is simple and rational. He has also referred at various places to the commentaries by Sri Aurobindo, Lokmanya Tilak, Vinoba, Dr Radhakrishnan and others. On a majority of occasions I found Sri Aurobindo's commentary the best, and sometimes that of Tilak, Vinoba or others.

Satyavratji divides the 18 chapters of the *Gita* into three parts. The first part deals with the first six chapters relating to *Karma* (action), the second part covers the next six chapters relating to *Bhakti* (devotion); and the last part embraces the remaining six that deal with *Jnana* (knowledge). However he says that these *yogas* or paths are not different from one another. Only, special emphasis has been laid on one out of three in each part, but the remaining two are also dealt with in it.

October 16

Have written to the Home Secretary regarding interviews with friends (copy given below) :

Chandigarh
16-10-75

To
The Home Secretary,
Government of India,
New Delhi

Sir,

I am glad that a detenu is now allowed one interview per week, and further that in special circumstances his friends may also see him.

As I have written to you before, this place is so far away from my home State that it is not possible for my relations to visit me every week. In the past week, for instance, none was able to come.

I, therefore, request that in such a special circumstance (in which I am likely to be deprived of the right of interview in a particular week) a friend may be allowed to interview me. With this in view I am giving below a brief list of my friends, excluding those who are in active politics :

1. Gangasharan Sinha, Patna
2. A. C. Sen, New Delhi
3. Ajit Bhattacharjea, New Delhi
4. Rameshwar Thakur, New Delhi
5. T. Abraham, Patna
6. Jainarayan Sahaya, Patna
7. S. Dasgupta, Varanasi
8. Krishnaraj Mehta
9. Narottam Shah, Bombay
10. Kusum Deshpande, Paunar, Wardha.

I have given these names without any reference to them, so I do hope they will suffer in no way for being my friends.

Yours sincerely,
JAYAPRAKASH NARAYAN

Mrs Gandhi's march onward to her personal dictatorship has reached another landmark. Saviour of democracy indeed! The latest amendment to MISA deprives the detenu of the right to be told the grounds of his detention; and, what is even more drastic, even the Court cannot ask the Government to supply to it such grounds. The lawyers have been arguing about the 'basic structure' of the Constitution, which according to the Supreme Court's judgment in the Kesavananda Bharati case was not subject to abridgement or damage through an amendment of the Constitution by Parliament. What can be more 'basic' to the structure of our Constitution than the citizen's right to move the courts to determine whether the citizen has been deprived of his freedom in accordance with the law or the *caprice* of the Government? What little had been left of the citizen's fundamental rights has been extinguished by the latest amendments. The reason is that the Courts have been trying to ascertain the grounds of a complainant's detention under MISA. Obviously, the Government had no valid and sufficient grounds for the detention of a large number, may be the vast majority of detenus. So, in order to save themselves from embarrassment, it has barred the Courts from enquiring into the grounds of detention. How convenient for the Government! Mrs Gandhi will no doubt go on protesting to Western correspondents her abiding faith in democracy and her desire to lift the Emergency as soon as the 'situation improved' and 'certain persons' who had been bent upon doing 'certain things' had changed their mind.

Anil [55] came—this time alone—yesterday. (October 17) Raja might be coming in the first week of November. Anil said that they had told Lal Babu that the first week of every month should be reserved for them, the remaining three weeks being divided between Calcutta and Patna according to convenience. This is a satisfactory arrangement.

55. J P's nephew.

October 19

Tarkunde came today. My case is still undecided.

He thought the latest amendment to MISA had made the task of the Supreme Court more difficult. I asked if the judgment (on Mrs Gandhi's appeal and Mr Rajnarain's cross-appeal) would be divided. He thought the Chief Justice would try hard for a unanimous judgment. In any case, he thought the judgment may strike down some clauses of the electoral law amendment (passed earlier by Parliament) but that Mrs Gandhi's election would remain unaffected. His main reason was that Mrs Gandhi had got the electoral law amended so as to allow a considerable latitude to government servants in working for the election of a minister or deputy minister. It is remarkable and shameful how Mrs Gandhi has played havoc with the laws of the land to suit her personal interests !

October 20

It was refreshing to read (*Tribune*, October 20) Sheikh Abdullah's open and bold speech while declaring his re-entry as a member of the National Conference. At least there is one person in the country who can talk straight like this to the PM. Maybe there are others and perhaps they do speak but their statements seem to be strictly blacked out from the press. Perhaps, when Parliament opens and the press is allowed to be present and to publish the proceedings truthfully, we shall hear more such voices. For the present, however, there is silence of the grave in the entire country.

(Translated from Hindi)   October 20

Economic revolution includes technological, industrial and agricultural revolutions, accompanied by a radical change in the pattern of ownership and management. It is not necessary that ownership and management always mean state ownership and state management. Ownership may vest in the State, in an individual or company of individuals, in a registered or co-operative society, or it may be a combination of all these forms. Also, ownership may vest in a local community, such as village assembly (gram sabha), assembly of a group of villages, block-level assembly (prakhand sabha), district council (zilla parishad), etc., or a combination of these forms of ownership, that is, of the local community and other patterns described above. There can be consumers' or producers' ownership and a combination of these and other, aforesaid patterns of ownership.

October 26

Pranav Chatterjee [56] (Patna), Goyal [57] (Delhi), both lawyers came to see me. It was a day of great happiness. Completed four months' detention today.

October 29

Have gone through hell these last days—continuous pain in the lower abdominal region. Felt miserable. All kinds of investigations were done but nothing has been found. Yet the pain, though less than before, continues. Constipation—*trifala* does not work anymore. Vomiting last night and this morning too. Have no appetite. There is total aversion to food.

November 2

The abdominal pain continues until this day. No appetite and aversion to food. No motion. Was moved to the hospital (the

56. Socialist leader and advocate.
57. D. R. Goyal, a noted advocate.

same room in which I was before) on 31st October night. Feel miserable and depressed due to this constant pain. They had X-rayed the lower intestines 3-4 days before (when I was still in the Bungalow). Barium meal enema was given. Today they will most probably X-ray the upper intestines (barium meal by mouth).

November 4

Feel better today. Abdominal pain is much less. Yesterday was Diwali. Tarkunde came. Told me about my case. It seems much depends on Mrs Padma Desai's [58] petition for permission for Morarjibhai's *friends* also to interview him. It seems the Court has decided in her favour; letters can also be written to friends. This I will do tomorrow if I am better.

58. Daughter-in-law of Morarji Desai.

Appendices

1. Letter addressed to the Prime Minister dated July 21, 1975

2. Letter addressed to the Prime Minister dated September 2, 1975

3. Letter addressed to the Prime Minister dated September 17, 1975

4. Letter addressed to Sheikh Mohamed Abdullah dated September 22, 1975

5. Message to the Nation

6. Hindi text

Appendix 1

Chandigarh
July 21, 1975

Dear Prime Minister,

I am appalled at press reports of your speeches and interviews. (The very fact that you have to say something everyday to justify your action implies a guilty conscience.) Having muzzled the press and every kind of public dissent, you continue with your distortions and untruths without fear of criticism or contradiction. If you think that in this way you will be able to justify yourself in the public eye and damn the Opposition to political perdition, you are sorely mistaken. If you doubt this, you may test it by revoking the Emergency, restoring to the people their fundamental rights, restoring the freedom of the press, releasing all those whom you have imprisoned or detained for no other crime than performing their patriotic duty. Nine years, Madam, is not a short period of time for the people, who are gifted with a sixth sense, to have found you out.

The burden of your song, as I have been able to discover, is that (a) there was a plan to paralyse the government, and (b) that one person had been trying to spread disaffection among the ranks of the civil and military forces. These seem to be your major notes. But there have been also minor notes. Every now and then you have been doling out your *obiter dicta*, such as the nation being more important than democracy and about the suitability of social democracy to India, and more in the same vein.

As I am the villain of the piece, let me put the record straight. This may be of no interest to you—for all your distortions and untruths are wilful and deliberate—but at least the truth would have been recorded.

About the plan to paralyse the government. There was no such plan and you know it. Let me state the facts.

Of all the States of India it was in Bihar alone where there was a people's movement. But there too, according to the Chief Minister's many statements, it had fizzled out long ago, if it had ever existed. But the truth is—and you should know if your ubiquitous Intelligence has served you right—that it was spreading and percolating deep down in the countryside. Until the time of my arrest janata sarkars were being formed from the village upwards to the block level. Later on, the process was to be taken up, hopefully, to the district and State level.

If you have cared to look into the programme of the janata sarkars, you would have found that for the most part it was constructive, such as : regulating the public distribution system, checking corruption at the lower levels of administration, implementing the land reform laws, settling disputes through the age-old custom of conciliation and arbitration, assuring a fair deal to Harijans, curbing such social evils as *tilak* and *dahez*, etc. There was nothing in all this that by any stretch of the imagination could be called subversive. Only where the janata sarkars were solidly organised were such programmes as non-payment of taxes taken up. At the peak of the movement in urban areas an attempt was made for some days, through *dharna* and picketing, to stop the working of government offices. At Patna whenever the Assembly opened attempts were made to persuade the members to resign and to prevent them peacefully from going in. All these were calculated programmes of civil disobedience, and thousands of men and women were arrested all over the State.

If all this adds up to an attempt to paralyse the Bihar government, well, it was the same kind of attempt as was made during the freedom struggle through non-co-operation and satyagraha to paralyse the British government. But that was a government established by force, whereas the Bihar government and the legislature are both constitutionally established bodies. What right has anyone to ask an elected government and elected legislature to go ? This is one of your favourite questions. But it has been answered umpteen times by competent persons, including well-known constitutional lawyers. The answer is that in a democracy the people do have the right to ask for the resignation of an elected government if it has gone corrupt and has been misruling. And if there is a legislature that persists in supporting

102

such a government it too must go, so that the people might choose better representatives.

But in that case how can it be determined what the people want? In the usual democratic manner. In the case of Bihar, the mammoth rallies and processions held in Patna, the thousands of constituency meetings held all over the state, the three-day Bihar *bandh*, the memorable happenings of the 4th November and the 'largest ever' meeting held at the Gandhi maidan on November 18 were a convincing measure of the people's will. And what had the Bihar government and Congress to show on their side? The miserable counter-offensive of November 16 which had been master-minded by Mr Borooah and on which according to reliable reports, the fantastic sum of 60 lakhs of rupees was spent. But if that was not conclusive enough proof, I had asked repeatedly for a plebiscite. But you were afraid to face the people.

While I am on the Bihar movement, let me mention another important point that would illumine the politics of such a type of movement. The students of Bihar did not start their movement just off the beat as it were. After formulating their demands at a conference they had met the Chief Minister and the Education Minister. They had had several meetings. But unfortunately the inept and corrupt Bihar government did not take the students seriously. Then the latter *gheraoed* the Assembly. The sad events of that day precipitated the Bihar movement. Even then the students did not demand the resignation of the Ministry nor the dissolution of the Assembly. It was after several weeks during which firing, lathi charges and indiscriminate arrests took place that the Students' Action Committee felt compelled to put up that demand. It was at that point that the Rubicon was crossed.

Thus, in Bihar, the government was given a chance to settle the issues across the table. None of the demands of the students was unreasonable or non-negotiable. But the Bihar government preferred the method of struggle, i.e., unparalleled repression. It was the same in UP. In either case the government rejected the path of negotiation, of trying to settle the issue across the table, and chose the path of strife. Had it been otherwise, there would have been no movement at all.

I have pondered over this riddle: why did not those governments act wisely ? The conclusion I have arrived at is that the main hurdle has been corruption. Somehow the governments have been unable to deal with corruption in their ranks, particularly at the top level : the ministerial level itself. And corruption has been the central point of the movement, particularly corruption in the government and the administration.

Be that as it may, except for Bihar there was no movement of its kind in any other State of India. In U.P. though Satyagraha had started in April, it was far from becoming a people's movement. In some other States though struggle committees had been formed, there seemed to be no possibility of a mass movement anywhere. And as the general election to the Lok Sabha was drawing near, the attention of the Opposition parties was turned more towards the coming electoral struggle than to any struggle involving civil disobedience.

Thus, the plan of which you speak, the plan to paralyse the government, is a figment of your imagination thought up to justify your totalitarian measures.

But suppose I grant you for a minute, for argument's sake, that there was such a plan, do you honestly believe that your erstwhile colleague, the former Deputy Prime Minister of India,* and Chandrashekhar, a member of the Congress Working Committee, were also a party to it ? Then why have they also been arrested and many others like them ?

No, dear Prime Minister, there was no plan to paralyse the government. If there was any plan, it was a simple, innocent and short-time plan to continue until the Supreme Court decided your appeal. It was this plan that was announced at the Ramlila grounds by Nanaji Deshmukh on 25th June and which was the subject matter of my speech that evening. The programme was for a selected number of persons to offer Satyagraha before or near your residence in support of the demand that you should step down until the Supreme Court's judgment on your appeal. The programme was to continue for seven days in Delhi, after which it was to be taken up in the States. And, as I have said above, it was to last only until the judgment of the Supreme Court. I do not see what is subversive or dangerous about it.

* Mr Morarji Desai.

In a democracy the citizen has an inalienable right to civil disobedience when he finds that other channels of redress or reform have dried up. It goes without saying that the Satyagrahi willingly invites and accepts his lawful punishment. This is the new dimension added to democracy by Gandhi. What an irony that it should be obliterated in Gandhi's own India !

It should be noted—and it is a very important point—that even this programme of Satyagraha would not have occurred to the Opposition had you remained content with quietly clinging on to your office. But you did not do it. Through your henchmen you had rallies and demonstrations organised in front of your residence begging you not to resign. You addressed these rallies and justifying your stand advanced spurious arguments and heaped calumny on the head of the Opposition. An effigy of the High Court Judge* was burnt before your residence and posters appeared in the city suggesting some kind of link between the judge and the CIA. When such despicable happenings were taking place every day, the Opposition had no alternative but to counteract the mischief. And how did it decide to do it ? Not by rowdyism but by orderly *Satyagraha*, self-sacrifice.

It was this 'plan' and not any imaginary plan to paralyse the government that has aroused your ire and cost the people their liberties and dealt a death-blow to their democracy.

And why has the freedom of the press been suppressed ? Not because the Indian press was irresponsible, dishonest or antigovernment. In fact, nowhere, under conditions of freedom, is the press more responsible, reasonable and fair than it has been in India. The truth is that your anger against it was aroused because on the question of your resignation, after the High Court's judgment, some of the papers took a line that was highly unpalatable to you. And when on the morrow of the Supreme Court judgment all the metropolitan papers, including the wavering *Times of India,* came out with well-reasoned and forceful editorials advising you to quit, freedom of the press became too much for you to stomach. That cooked the goose of the Indian press, and you struck your deadly blow. It staggers one's imagi-

* Mr Justice J. M. L. Sinha of the Allahabad High Court who delivered the judgment of June 12 disqualifying Mrs Gandhi from membership of parliament on the ground of corrupt election practices.

nation to think that so valuable a freedom of the press, the very life-breath of democracy, can be snuffed out because of the personal pique of a Prime Minister.

You have accused the Opposition of trying to lower the prestige and position of the country's Prime Minister. But in reality the boot is on the other leg. No one has done more to lower the position and prestige of that great office than yourself. Can one ever think of the Prime Minister of a democratic country who cannot even vote in his parliament because he has been found guilty of corrupt electoral practices? (The Supreme Court may reverse the High Court's judgment—most probably it will, in this atmosphere of terror—but as long as that is not done your guilt and your deprivation of right to vote remain.)

As for the 'one person' who is supposed to have tried to sow disaffection in the armed and police forces, he denies the charge. All that he has done is to make the men and officers of the Forces conscious of their duties and responsibilities. Whatever he has said in that connection is within the law : the Constitution, the Army Act and the Police Act.

So much for your major points : the plan to paralyse the government and the attempt to sow disaffection in the armed and police forces. Now a few of your minor points and *obiter dicta.*

You are reported to have said that democracy is not more important than the nation. Are you not presuming too much Madam Prime Minister ? You are not the only one who cares for the nation. Among those whom you have detained or imprisoned there are many who have done much more for the nation than you. And everyone of them is as good a patriot as yourself. So, please do not apply salt to our wounds by lecturing to us about the nation.

Moreover, it is a false choice that you have formulated. There is no choice between democracy and the nation. It was for the good of the nation that the people of India declared in their Constituent Assembly on 26th November 1949 that "We, the people of India, having solemnly resolved to constitute India into a Sovereign Democratic Republic . . . give to ourselves this Constitution". That democratic Constitution cannot be changed into a totalitarian one by a mere ordinance or law of Parliament. That can be done only by the people of India themselves in their new Constituent Assembly, especially elected for that specific purpose. If Justice, Liberty, Equality and Fraternity have not been rendered to 'all its citizens' even after a quarter of a century of signing of that Constitution, the fault is not that of the Constitution or of democracy but of the Congress party that has been in power in Delhi all these years. It is precisely because of that failure that there is so much unrest among the people and the youth. Repression is no remedy for that. On the other hand, it only compounds the failure.

I, no doubt, see that the papers are full these days of reports of new policies, new drives, show of new enthusiasm. Apparently you are trying to make up for lost time, that is to say, you are making a show of doing here and now what you failed to do in nine years. But your twenty points will go the same way as your ten points did and the 'Stray Thoughts'*. But I assure you this time the people will not be fooled. And I assure you of another thing too : a party of self-seekers and spineless opportunists and *jee-huzurs* ('yesmen') such as the Congress, alas, has become, can never do anything worthwhile. (Not all Congressmen are such. There are quite a few exceptions, such as those who have been deprived of their party membership and some of them their freedom. So that according to the *dharma* of totalitarianism, there could be no criticism even within the party.) There will be a lot of propaganda and make-ado on paper but on the ground level the situation will not change the least. The condition of the poor—and they are the great majority over the greater part of the country—has been worsening over the past years. It would be enough if the downward trend were arrested. But, for that your whole approach to politics and economics will have to change.

I have written the above in utter frankness without mincing words. I have done so not out of anger or so as to get even with you in words. No, that would be a show of impotence. Nor does it show any lack of appreciation for the care that is being taken of my health. I have done it only to place the

* This refers to the note on economic policy that Mrs Gandhi sent to the AICC meeting held at Bangalore in July 1969.

naked truth before you, which you have been trying to cover up and distort.

Having performed this unpleasant duty, may I conclude with a few parting words of advice ? You know I am an old man. My life's work is done. And after Prabha's going I have nothing and no one to live for. My brother and nephew have their family and my younger sister—the elder one died years ago—has her sons and daughters. I have given all my life, after finishing education, to the country and asked for nothing in return. So I shall be content to die a prisoner under your regime.

Would you listen to the advice of such a man ? Please do not destroy the foundations that the Fathers of the Nation, including your noble father, had laid down. There is nothing but strife and suffering along the path that you have taken. You inherited a great tradition, noble values and a working democracy. Do not leave behind a miserable wreck of all that. It would take a long time to put all that together again. For it would be put together again, I have no doubt. A people who fought British imperalism and humbled it cannot accept indefinitely the indignity and shame of totalitarianism. The spirit of man can never be vanquished, no matter how deeply suppressed. In establishing your personal dictatorship you have buried it deep. But it will rise from the grave. Even in Russia it is slowly coming up.

You have talked of social democracy. What a beautiful image those words call to the mind. But you have seen in eastern and central Europe how ugly the reality is. Naked dictatorship and, in the ultimate analysis, Russian overlordship. Please, please do not push India toward that terrible fate.

And may I ask to what purpose all these draconian measures ? In order to be able to carry out your twenty points ? But who was preventing you from carrying out the ten points ? All the discontent, the protest, the Satyagraha were due precisely to the fact that you were not doing anything to implement your programme, inadequate as it was, to lighten the misery and burden under which the people and youth were groaning. This is what Chandrashekhar, Mohan Dharia, Krishna Kant and their friends have been saying for which they have been punished.

You have talked of 'drift' in the country. But was that due

to Opposition or to me ? The drift was because of your lack of decision, direction and drive. You seem to act swiftly and dramatically only when your personal position is threatened. Once that is assured, the drift begins. Dear Indiraji, please do not identify yourself with the nation. You are not immortal, India is.

You have accused the Opposition and me of every kind of villainy. But let me assure you that if you do the right things, for instance, your 20-points, tackling corruption at Ministerial levels, electoral reforms, etc., take the Opposition into confidence, heed its advice, you will receive the willing co-operation of every one of us. For that you need not destroy democracy. The ball is in your court. It is for you to decide.

With these parting words, let me bid you farewell. May God be with you.

Yours sincerely
JAYAPRAKASH

Appendix 2

(Draft of letter to PM which, may or may not be sent
—to be decided by me later.)*

Dear Prime Minister,

It is after a great deal of hesitation that I am writing to you again. I am doing so because I feel much worried about our country. The Fathers of Indian freedom had the great wisdom to establish a democratic sovereign republic. Of the three words, the democratic is the most important. A country that had just fought for and won its independence could not be sovereign. There also could not be any question of any kind of monarchy being established. The country had naturally to be sovereign and it had naturally to be a republic. But there was no natural reason why it must be also democratic. There are several sovereign republics in the world that are *not democratic*. Sovereignty and republicanism were not matters of choice. The country in the circumstances could not but be sovereign and republican.

But a sovereign republic could be a dictatorship—either of a person or a party caucus or a military junta; it could be an oligarchy, or again it could be based on a restricted franchise, say, restricted to the educated (the word 'educated' being defined variously). But our Fathers chose a parliamentary democracy based on adult franchise. This was a great leap forward. And it drew the admiration and acclaim of the world.

As I have written elsewhere, adult suffrage based on parliamentary democracy was made possible only because the genius of Mahatma Gandhi fashioned a form of struggle for independence which allowed the full participation of the masses including the humblest and even children. Crores of people openly took part in processions and meetings, hartals and morchas and lakhs

* The letter was not sent to the Prime Minister. See entry for September 4, 1975.

were in prison. Given this mass base—the mass awakening, the mass participation—democracy on the basis of adult franchise became a possibility and then a reality. It is also because of the same mass involvement that Indian democracy had survived (until June 25, 1975) despite wars, famines, floods, growing and expanding poverty and growing unemployment, and not the least, MISEDUCATION.

It was not just a political proposition, a political ideal but it became a reality. If India had not won freedom this way, there was much less chance of parliamentary democracy being established. The most likely result would have been dictatorship.

Now for the first time since the promulgation of the Democratic Sovereign Republic Constitution more than 25 years ago the democratic structure of our country has been grievously—one hopes not fatally—damaged. This is a matter of deep and growing concern for me. And it is this concern that drives me to write this letter.

The Emergency proclamation and all that has followed since have been justified on the ground of 'danger of internal disturbance'. (Parenthetically, I may remark that the first emergency that was proclaimed in view of external danger still continues, though no external danger exists today in spite of Pakistan's anti-India propaganda. That is nothing new and certainly does not constitute an imminent military danger from Pakistan.) As for the danger of internal disturbance, Madam Prime Minister, it is my sober and objective view that at the end of June last there was no danger of internal disturbance—let me take State by State—in Jammu & Kashmir (if there was any, it was no more than a law and order problem with which Sheikh Sahib was quite competent to deal according to the laws in force and MISA); there was no such danger in Punjab, in Haryana, in Chandigarh UT,* in Delhi UT, in UP, in spite of the limited Satyagraha that was going on), in MP, in Gujarat, in West Bengal, in Maharashtra, in Andhra Pradesh, in Orissa, in Assam, in Karnataka, in Tamil Nadu, in Kerala. In the extreme eastern States, Nagaland and the others, the disturbances were not new and they were claimed to be under control. In any case, the

* Union Territory.

Governor there had special powers and the Army was on the spot.

Only in Bihar you might claim there was not only a danger of, but actual disturbance. You and I would differ on this point and I would not want to argue about it here. But accepting your own premise, why should the whole country suffer on account of the faults of just one State ? If you wished, the Emergency could have been proclaimed for Bihar alone. Even the British used to do it restricting their special laws to the States where the Civil Disobedience movement was strong and extending them to other States as and when needed.

Anyhow, all that is in the past. Rightly or wrongly, the Emergency was applied to the whole country. But what is the position now ? You yourself have claimed several times, and so have your colleagues, that everything is quiet now, that there is no trace of any agitation or the movement to be seen anywhere. It certainly appears to be so from the press and other reports. If that is so then why are thousands of men and women detained without trial ? What crime, what offence ? Why is Morarjibhai still held in detention and why the Congress Working Committee member Chandrashekhar and Congress Parliamentary Party Secretary Ramdhan ? Why so many others ? Thousands of them. If they are guilty, please have them tried and let the law take its course. Why should the Emergency continue to suffocate the freedom of citizens, the freedom of the press and go on with the whole sordid affair ? Are you afraid that once the Emergency is revoked, the lid will be off—the genii of disturbance will spring up again ? If you are, I must say you are afraid of shadows. Why must you and your party take upon itself the burden of this terrible wrong ? Do you think it will do you or your party any good ? You may want to frighten the people, cow them down, teach them a lesson. But history has shown that this never works. Action and reaction are equal and opposite not only in physics but also in politics.

In your interviews with pressmen, particularly, foreign pressmen or other news media, you have reaffirmed your resolve to hold the General Elections, but have refused to indicate the time. In one interview you are reported to have said that you are watching the Opposition leaders and you think that they have not yet changed 'their stand'. What is the stand that you want them to change ? Do you want them to stop to function as Opposition parties ? Obviously you cannot want anything that is so absurd, because that would be nonsense. Then what ? You want them perhaps to be balanced ? But, Madam, have you yourself set a good example ? What vitriol have you not poured over their heads ? The most unworthy and unsubstantiated charge you have been making against them, not sparing me either, is that those whose are opposed to you have some kind of dubious link with foreign powers. You have been challenged many times to prove your words or stop your insinuations. But so far you have produced no proof, but the insinuations still continue to be repeated on suitable occasions. God knows whom you are trying to deceive. And the great joke is that you yourself and your party—much to the disgust of many leading members of your party—are hand in glove with the (Rightist) CPI, who are stooges of Soviet Russia. In your own party leadership there are dupes who are little better than stooges of the Soviets.

I know this would be jumped upon as an anti-Soviet gambit and divert the whole argument from the main point I am making here. You should know better. I believe no less than anyone in India remaining on the friendliest possible terms with the Soviet Union. But friendship should never be servitude. India should never become a satellite nation. It is in our national interest that we should be friendly to Soviet Russia, but we should be careful that we do not pass over into Russia's 'sphere of influence'. Sometimes I fear that we are already within that zone, whether knowingly or unknowingly. The Russians certainly seem very keen to prod you forward on to the path of totalitarianism. The latest evidence of this is their whole-hearted support to your recent anti-democratic steps.

Today, dear Prime Minister, let me repeat there is no internal disturbance anywhere in sight nor any—and this is important—danger of internal disturbance in any of the States in India. Not even in Bihar any more, even if one were to concede for argument's sake that there was any danger of *disturbance*. (A civil disobedience movement is not a civil disturbance, but I shall not argue that point because I cannot hope to carry conviction with you.) All I wish to say is that in view of the unparalleled tragedy of Patna and some other parts of Bihar, no one connected

114

with my movement (if I may call it 'my', only because it has come to be looked upon as such) can ever think of trying to revive the movement. At this moment of pain and suffering, disease and death, deprivation and hunger no one can think of a struggle or movement. Our only duty is to serve and succour the people and, most important of all, to help the people to help themselves. And if I were free this is the lead I would have given. Lest you should think that I have cooked up this argument only to persuade you to alter your present course, it is not so. I gave the same lead at the time of the Bihar famine of 1966-67, when Sarvodaya work was suspended and at another time (in 1961) when parts of Monghyr and Nawadah districts which never had known floods before were suddenly inundated on account of unprecedented rain in the nearby hills. I gave the same advice and myself gave up all Sarvodaya work and plunged into the work of relief. That was the occasion when I saw dead bodies floating in the rice-paddies, and the stink filling the air.

There is also another important point to consider. When the Bihar movement had started in 1974 February-March, the Assembly elections were full three years away (1977 February-March) and not just around the corner as it is being made out now. The Lok Sabha elections were also full two years distant. Now the Lok Sabha elections are only six months away (and maybe the Assembly elections also if you so decide). For the Opposition parties, if their leaders were to be freed and the parties were to be allowed to function, the most important task, besides the immediate task of rendering relief, would be to prepare for the elections. They can have no interest, even if I or anyone else were so foolish as to attract them to reactivisation of the movement; they would have no interest in it whatever. The attitude of the students would be the same.

So, to sum up, now that you claim to have the situation under control and there is no anti-Government agitation or movement of any kind, and now that there is calm and order throughout the country, and further that you profess faith in parliamentary democracy and the scheduled parliamentary elections are due six months hence, you should in all fairness to yourself, to the country and to democracy, order the release of all those detained at present on political grounds (I am not concerned about the

Appendix 3

Dear Prime Minister,

On 27th August I had made my request for a month's parole. On the 4th September Mr Vorah of the Union Ministry of Agriculture came here to post me with all that was being done to render relief to the people of Patna. (He did not tell me anything about the rural areas.) I expressed to him my satisfaction over the steps taken by you and your government. At the same time I told him that after his account my desire to be allowed to serve the people had grown keener and more urgent. I requested him to communicate that to Professor P. N. Dhar, at whose instance he had come to see me.

It was natural of me to deduce from Mr Vorah's visit that my request for parole was being taken seriously and a decision would soon be reached, particularly in view of the extreme urgency of the situation. But I am sorry to say that three whole weeks have been allowed to pass, weeks during which waves after recurring waves of floods in different parts of Bihar have caused me deep mental agony. My part of Uttar Pradesh has also been repeatedly flooded, and I have no news of my own village and home. Yesterday's *Tribune* in a three-column headline said, 'Bihar floods take grim turn'. This morning again (17-9-75) the paper reports, 'Bihar Flood Situation Deteriorates'. The breaching of the right bank of the main Kosi Canal is no small matter. The sudden and widespread destruction must be indescribable. Hundreds of Monghyr villages are under water. This year's calamity seems to have surpassed even that of the Great Earthquake.

In these circumstances, I cannot but renew my request to be given a chance to serve the people. Please do not let politics come in the way. Even the British had humanity enough in the event of a calamity to set at liberty those who were fighting to destroy their empire. What place can politics have in a situation of such staggering human suffering? For my part, I cannot do better than quote from my letter to the Deputy Commissioner, Chandigarh (31-8-75), the contents of which were to be passed on to the proper authorities in New Delhi. I wrote *inter alia*: 'I would consider it immoral and impolitic to exploit the period of freedom allowed to me for any political purpose. Indeed to talk of politics at this moment would be to mock the miseries and sufferings of the people. No one with a grain of human sympathy would ever think of doing such a thing.' This continues to be my stand.

It cannot be government's case that there was no need of voluntary relief services. You yourself and some of your colleagues have appealed for voluntary agencies to help. As for my own competence for relief work, you have some personal knowledge to go by.

I had given Mr Vorah another message for Professor Dhar, namely, that the Bihar flood situation had created a good opportunity for government to review and revise the entire political policy it has followed since and prior to the proclamation of the Emergency. This conviction of mine has grown stronger since. Not only has the Bihar flood situation worsened, but there have also been floods in most parts of the country. There can be no question of anyone starting a movement or struggle at such a time. The political emergency, granting that it existed at any time, has passed and its place has been taken by an emergency of human suffering, calling for a national effort. No less a person than the Union Home Minister has declared the other day at Madras that there was *normalcy prevailing throughout the country* (His actual words : *'With normalcy prevailing throughout the country* 30 per cent of those arrested have been released'! PTI, *Tribune,* 14-9-75). What justification can there be now for prolonging the emergency ?

There is also another reason, a much more important one, why the emergency must end. It is the drawing near of the parliamentary elections. According to the Constitution, elections to the Lok Sabha must be held early next year. On the pretext of a non-existent emergency the term of the present Lok Sabha might be extended. But you know how flimsy that pretext would be. It would deceive no one, and you would have permanently given the go-by to parliamentary democracy, by which you swear so ardently in public, and in the end the loss would be yours more than anyone else's. On what ground can you deny the people their democratic right to choose their new representatives to the Lok Sabha ? Who except your sycophants will believe that you are taking this grave step because there is an emergency in the country ?

It is the third week of September now. By the end of this month or the beginning of the next, you should announce in unambiguous terms that elections to the Lok Sabha would be held early in 1976 and that the Election Commission would fix the dates in due course. You will find, Madam, that that single announcement by you would work a miraculous change in the political climate of the country. In a democracy, a General Election (provided it is fair and free) acts like a powerful catharsis, cleansing the political atmosphere, easing tensions and bringing health and vigour to the body politic.

Praying for a dispassionate consideration of the suggestions made above, and with best wishes.

Yours sincerely,
JAYAPRAKASH

Appendix 4

My dear Sheikh Saheb,

In this morning's *Tribune* (September 22) a PTI report from Srinagar is headlined 'Sheikh Favours Conciliation at All-India Level'. I was naturally interested, and carefully read that report twice. The agency report says, *inter alia*, the following (Words within single quotes are the correspondent's and those within double quotes are reported to be yours) :

'He declined direct,comment on reports of his mediatory efforts appearing in the Western press, saying he wishes such differences to be resolved in a spirit of conciliation.'

'When correspondents persisted in their attempts to draw him out ... the Sheikh said his services were always at the disposal of the Prime Minister. "It all depends on the situation.... One must wait for the appropriate time", he said.'

Further on, 'He said it was a "delicate task" and a "delicate subject" for one to dwell on and emphasised that "everyone would like normalcy to be restored". He added that as far as he claimed to know the wishes of the Prime Minister, "she is more than keen to end the Emergency. It all depends on the overall situation." '

Coming from a friend like you, with so much of goodwill in both camps, and occupying such an important position as you do, your words are of extraordinary significance and interest for me.

I whole-heartedly reciprocate your view that differences, such as we had with the government, should be resolved in a spirit of conciliation. But, Sheikh Saheb, there never was any discussion on the main issues raised by the movement : corruption in politics, government and administration; electoral reforms so as to make elections less expensive, fair, free and more representative of the people's will as expressed through the ballot box; radical educational reform; urgent economic measures to tackle unemploy-

ment (educated and uneducated), etc. We had put forward concrete proposals in regard to these issues. But the Prime Minister
showed no inclination to have them discussed around the table
in a spirit of conciliation. When the Tarkunde Committee on
electoral reforms submitted its interim report, I invited organisa-
tional as well as parliamentary leaders of all the political parties
represented in Parliament to discuss them and, if possible, work
out agreed proposals. The Congress and the CPI declined to
attend. In such a situation how could differences be resolved in
a spirit of conciliation?

Only on one occasion, on 1 November 1974, the Prime Minister
invited me to discuss the Bihar movement. There was no agreement between us on the question of dissolution of the Bihar
Assembly. I was prepared to accept her formula of suspension of
the Assembly, *provided* the Assembly did not re-convene before
the next elections and President's rule was continued until then.
This proviso was not acceptable to her. That same day she declared at a public meeting that the issue would be decided at
the next elections. I accepted her challenge and there the matter
rested. Meanwhile the repression continued. Three days later, on
4 November, I along with others was tear-gassed and lathi-charged.
You know the rest of the story.

If you remember, Chandrashekhar, Ram Dhan, Mohan
Dharia, Krishna Kant and their friends were saying exactly what
you have said in your interview: that the issues posed by the
(JP) movement should be settled across the table and not by
repression. For that, you know what has been done to them.

Since our arrest and the proclamation of Emergency, we have
been victims of all manner of distortions, slanders, even outright
lies. I shall give you only one example—the latest sample of
these. Speaking at the First Conference of Educators (*sic*) in
Secularism, Socialism and Democracy, the Prime Minister, irked
by the vocal concern of the Western press over the eclipse of
Indian democracy, asked hysterically: 'Would this country be
considered more democratic had a large number of people been
killed after June 29,* if I myself, my family and the Chief

---

* It was on June 29 that the proposed week-long Satyagraha was
to begin.

Ministers and others who support me had been annihilated ? '

That the Prime Minister of a great country should descend so low and attempt in such a cynical manner to spread hatred and hostility against her political opponents in incredible. But there it is in cold print.

However, in spite of all that has happened and is happening, I am prepared to seek the path of conciliation. I shall, therefore, be much obliged if you kindly see me as soon as possible so that I could discuss this matter with you. I being the villain of the piece, the arch-conspirator, culprit number one, a return to true normalcy, not the false one established by repression and terror, can only be brought about with my co-operation. I am herewith offering you my full co-operation.

You have said that the PM is 'more than keen to end the Emergency'. Well, the first test of her keenness will be whether this letter is allowed to be delivered to you and whether you are permitted to see me.*

Looking forward to seeing you soon, and with most affectionate regards.

Yours as ever,
JAYAPRAKASH

* The letter was not delivered to Sheikh Mohammed Abdullah, nor was he allowed to call on J P.

Appendix 5

Message to the Nation*

Many friends have been pressing me in the past few months to say something to the nation. Being bedridden and therefore out of touch with the objective situation in the country, I have been hesitating to say anything. Only a few days ago the Prime Minister† spoke to the nation. After his excellent discourse, I should have thought there was no need for any other voice to be raised. But friends still think that the Prime Minister having spoken as head of the government, there was need for a common citizen like me to speak on behalf of the people. While I disclaim any authority to speak for the people, I am placing here my views as a common citizen.

The first observation that I should like to make and emphasise is that the results of the last general elections were due to the students' and people's movement that had started from Gujarat and spread to Bihar and whose message had resounded throughout the country. The essence of that message was that an elected representative of the people does not necessarily acquire a right to hold on to his position until the expiry of his legal term. The principle that was asserted during the movement was that if an individual representative, or a representative government, fail in his duty, became corrupt and oppressive and inefficient, the electors, i.e. the people had a right to demand his resignation irrespective of the time he may yet have left to serve. The example of ex-President Richard Nixon of the United States illustrates the proposition I am enunciating here.

It is true that what is called the 'right of recall' has no place in our Constitution, but in a democracy the people have an unwritten right which they can exercise if and when necessary.

All this does not mean that any small number of disgruntled

---

* Text of the Broadcast to the Nation on April 13, 1977.

† Mr. Morarji Desai.

persons have the right to demand an elected representative or government to step down from office whenever they wish. But it does mean that if it is found beyond any doubt that a vast majority of the people concerned are convinced of the corruption, nepotism and inefficiency of a government or an elected representative and demand their resignation, the people's voice must prevail. It is possible that the party in power, or the individual representative concerned, might also mobilise supporters, but if there is a genuine people's upsurge against them, democratic ethics and practice require that the will of the great majority must prevail over that of a small minority.

To the constitutionalists, this may appear to be an anarchic proposition. However, it should be remembered that practically every major constitution in the world was drafted in the wake of revolutionary upheavals.

This is a good occasion to look back and recall how the students' movement against corruption in Gujarat has assumed an all-India character. Political and governmental corruption was the central point of the people's movement. Therefore, it is the duty of those who have come to power in the wake of that movement to take some concrete and effective steps to stop and root out corruption from these spheres. It is my view that just like the High Courts and the Supreme Court, there should be an autonomous institution set up with legal authority and rights both at the Centre and in the States. The Swedish Ombudsman naturally comes to one's mind, but in Indian conditions some broader kind of institution seems to be necessary. For instance, at the Centre a body that may be known as Lok Pal might be set up consisting of not more than five members with powers to hold investigations on their own initiative as well as on the initiative of any citizen or any private or public body. A group of individual jurists might be entrusted with the task of drawing up a blueprint of such a body, and a clause to this effect might be inserted in the Constitution. These are my first expectations from the government.

The main issue raised by the students'-cum-people's movement was electoral and administrative reforms so as to make elections cheap and truly representative and bring the administration nearer to the people. Another important demand concerned educational reforms so as to relate education to the problems of the country and fit the educated to deal with them. It was also desired that a modicum of education should be made universal and illiteracy and ignorance banished from the land. The charter of demands that I placed before the speaker of the Lok Sabha and the President (chairman) of the Rajya Sabha on behalf of the people on March 6, 1975, deserves to be reproduced here so that it may serve as a standard by which to measure the work and functioning of the present government.

Except for the Centre, Congress governments still continue to function in the States. It is necessary as soon as possible to give a chance to the people to elect their fresh representatives who would be committed to the people's charter in addition to their election manifestos.

It will be recalled that the ultimate objective of the people's movement was defined by me as total revolution. This term 'total revolution' was derided by some at that time and brushed aside by some others as a dream of an impractical person. Therefore, I should like to repeat my faith in what I called total revolution and pledge myself to work for it as soon as my health permits. In our heritage there are some things that are noble and valuable; they have to be preserved and strengthened. But we have also inherited a great deal of superstition and wrong values and unjust human and social relations. The caste system among the Hindus is a glaring example of our evil inheritance. From the time of Lord Buddha, and may be from even earlier times, attempts have been made to destroy the hierarchical system of caste but it still flourishes in every part of the country. It is time that we blotted out this black spot from the Hindu society and proclaimed and practised the equality and brotherhood of all men.

Similarly, there are rotten customs and manners associated with such things as marriage, birth, death, etc. The purging of these evils also falls within the purview of the total revolution.

Coming to more modern spheres of life, such as education, it is time that the radical recommendations of the several education commissions, the Kothari Commission not being the least of them, are implemented. Here we might follow the example of China in which all the schools and colleges were closed down and the students were sent out to the villages and slums of the towns to impart the rudiments of education to every citizen,. young or old.

I have not said anything here about the usual socio-economic reforms that are so much talked about, but about which so little has actually been done. For this task too, youth power can be drafted with advantage to the youth themselves and to society at large.

Finally, if God grants me better health in the coming months. I look forward to take up my cry of total revolution and do whatever might lie in my power. Meanwhile, thd work need not be stopped. Let everyone do his bit, singly or in co-operation with others. Here is a beacon light for our youth. I hope they will steer the course of their life towards that light. I am at their disposal even in my sick bed for advice and such guidance as I might be capable of giving.

So forward my young friends.

Sampoorna kranti ab nara hai.

Bhawi itihas hamara hai.

Index

Youth Worker released, 87, n50.
Parliament
  its Supremacy, 60 ff.
Parliamentary Democracy
  J P's suggestion for improvement,
  11
Patel, (Sardar) Vallabhbhai, 41, 71
Patil, S. K., 41
Patna, flood ravages, 35 ff; 51-52
Political Order
  systemic change without struggle,
  21
Prabhavati Devi, J P's wife, 10 n10
Prasad (Prof.), Ishwari, historian,
  13, 15
Prasad, Rajendra
  Bihar, Earthquake 1934 relief or-
  ganised, 38, 71
Prasad, Rajeshwar, J P's younger
  brother, Petition to Supreme
  Court for 'acceptable' company
  to J P, 5 n2.
Prasad, Shivnath (Lal Babu), J P's
  brother-in-law, 5 n4, 86, 94
Prashant, Sarvodaya Youth Activist
  in Bihar, released 87 n51
Prime Minister
  not direct election,12
Prohibition
  Tribune announces likely total
  implementation, 77

Radhakrishnan (Dr.) S., President of
  India, attends Rajen Babu's Fune-
  ral, 85
Raja, 86, 94
Rajgopalachari, C., 71
Ramachandran, M. G. leader, ADMK,
  · 84 n46
Ramdhan
  arrest of, 4, 71, 113
Ram, Jagjivan, 4, 77, 81
  on '20-point' plan', 77
Ram, Raja, DMK leader, 84 n44
Reddy, Brahmanand
  normalcy in the country, 68

Rehman, Mujibur
  regime in Bangladesh, 17-20
Representation of the People Act
  amendment to 8, 9, 28
Rukhaiyar (Mrs.), Sheela, Mahila
  Charkha Samiti Worker, 35 n24
Rule from a Single Centre cannot
  be indefinite, 16
Russell, Bertrand, 75

Sadat, Anwar, President, U.A.R.,
  J P on, 78
Saiyidan (Dr.), K. G., 75 n41
Sarva Seva Sangh, 7 n7
Satyadeva Paribrajak (Swami), 25
Satyavrat (Prof.)
  commentary on the Gita, 17
Schumachar, Fritz, 54-55, 63
Sehgal, Nayantara, Writer (Pt. J.
  Nehru's niece), 87 n52
Sen, A. C., J P's close associate, 19
  n19
Sezhiyan Era, DMK member, Lok
  Sabha, 84 n45
Shrimali (Dr.), K. L., "Educators"
  President, 71, 74, 75
Simha Shri Krishna, First Chief
  Minister Bihar, 41 n30
Singh (Sardar) Mohinder, Executive
  Magistrate flower bouquet to J P
  on Birthday, 90
Singh, Swaran, 4
Soviet Russia, 6-7
  backing to Mrs. Gandhi, 3-4
  silent on Bangladesh affairs, 20
  worry over West Asia Balance of
  Power, 53
Struggle against Government
  reasons, 41 ff.
Struggle for Freedom in India, 15
Students, need to understand them,
  66
Students' Movement, 23-25
Sudha, J P's younger sister's dau-
  ghter
  released, 86 n48

Tarkunde, V. M., 5 n3 54, 71
    meets J P, 94, 96
    on Mrs. Gandhi-Raj Narain Appeals, 94; and MISA amendment, 94
Total Revolution, 25, 42 ff.
    J P on, 33-35, 44, 87-88

Uma, Sudha's husband
    released, 86 n48
University Students
    in Movement, 48
United States of America
    arming Pakistan, 7

Vajpayee, A. B., 71
Vorah, B. B., Additional Secretary, Food & Agriculture Ministry
    on comprhensive use of water-management in Bihar, 50-51
    reports to J P on Patna floods, 49-50

Wolfe, Bertram
    quotation from *Khruschev and Stalin's Ghost*, 90

Young Turks, 4, 28
"Youth for Democracy", 10